ELIZABETH I

Neil Tonge
Series editor: Christopher Culpin

Longman

Edinburgh Gate
Harlow, Essex

CONTENTS

Part 1   Telling the story   3

Part 2

1 How successful was the Religious Settlement of 1559?   38
   Focus: Analysis of key features
   Tasks: Evaluation and interpretation of sources
         Writing essays

2 Elizabeth and her Parliaments – a marriage of
   convenience?   63
   Focus: Analysis of key features
   Tasks: Class exercise
         Essay writing

3 Foreign policy – national interest or Protestant
   crusade?   85
   Focus: Analysis of key features
   Tasks: Making notes
         Class exercise

4 Poverty and legislation – social concern or
   social control?   100
   Focus: Understanding of causation and motivation
   Tasks: Class exercise

5 Gloriana – a golden age?   117
   Focus: Understanding of interpretations
   Tasks: Interpretations

Further reading   124

Index   125

PART ONE

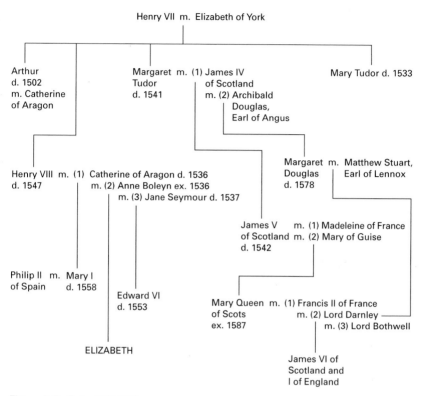

Figure 1 The Tudors 1485–1603

TELLING THE STORY

Between two and three o'clock in the morning of 24 March 1603 Elizabeth Tudor slowly slipped from life after refusing to eat or sleep for three weeks. For some observers she had outlived her greatness. John Clapham, a contemporary historian who watched Elizabeth's funeral procession without regret, recorded a bitter conclusion to her reign. The people of England and Wales, he claimed, 'could not be in a worse state than they were, considering that the people generally were much impoverished by continual subsidies and taxes'.

Yet during Elizabeth's considerable reign of 45 years, she had been not just popular but adulated as a goddess. The poet John Davies expressed the sentiments of many when he wrote in 1602:

This was the picture of her wondrous thought ...
And there did represent in lively show
Our glorious English court's divine image
As it should be in this our Golden Age.

John Davies, 'Hymn to Astrea' (1602) in **Anthology of Renaissance Verse** (Longman, 1978)

Historians are also divided in their judgements. Anne Somerset, in her 1991 biography *Elizabeth I*, is lavish in her praise of Elizabeth's achievements:

Under Elizabeth, the nation acquired its self-confidence and sense of direction. At a time when the authority of the majority of her fellow monarchs was under threat or in decline, she upheld the interests of the crown while not encroaching on those of her subjects, restored the coinage, and created a Church which, for all its failings, came close to being truly national. While many countries were rent by civil war ... she presided over a realm which (with the exception of the Irish dominions) was fundamentally stable and united ... Besides this, Elizabeth was responsible for raising England's international standing, defying the most powerful nation in Christendom.

A. Somerset, **Elizabeth I** (Weidenfeld and Nicolson, 1991)

Other historians are less flattering. Christopher Haigh, in his 1988 history *Elizabeth I*, describes her as a ruler overtaken by events:

Elizabeth died unloved and unlamented, and it was partly her own fault. She had aimed for popularity and political security by projecting herself as the ever-young and ever-beautiful virgin mother of her people ... she ended her days as an irascible old woman, presiding over war and failure abroad and poverty and factionalism at home. ... her reign had been 30 years of illusion followed by 15 years of disillusion.

C. Haigh, **Elizabeth I** (Macmillan, 1988)

The traditional picture of Elizabeth's reign as a 'golden age' contains much truth, but the whole truth, as always, is more complex.

As you read on, bear in mind these central questions:

◢ To what extent was Elizabeth 'the noblest queen that had ever lived'?
◢ Did her reign represent a 'golden age'?

In Part One you will find:

◢ a timeline of key events
◢ a summary of Elizabeth's early life before she became Queen
◢ a description of the making of Elizabeth's public image
◢ the judgement of historians on Elizabeth's government
◢ an analysis of the state of England during Tudor times
◢ a summary of the main phases of Elizabeth's reign.

Key events

1558	Elizabeth becomes Queen of England
1559	Religious Settlement based on Protestant principles
	Treaty of Cateau-Cambrésis ended war with France
1560	Intervention in Scotland on behalf of Protestants to oust the French
1562–3	Ill-fated attempt to support the French Protestants
1562–6	Vestment (Vestiarian) Controversy – Puritan attempt to abolish clergy's ceremonial dress
1566	Revolt in the Netherlands against Spanish domination
1568	Mary Queen of Scots escapes to England after a revolt of her leading noblemen. She hopes Elizabeth will restore her to her throne
1569	The Northern Rising – a plot to marry the Duke of Norfolk to Mary Queen of Scots, depose Elizabeth and restore Catholicism in England
1570	The Pope excommunicates Elizabeth
	Marriage negotiations with the Duke of Anjou
1571	The Ridolfi Plot – an attempt to depose Elizabeth with the help of Spain
1572	Norfolk executed for his part in the Ridolfi Plot
	Treaty of Blois with France – France agrees to withdraw support for Mary Queen of Scots and to end French influence in Scotland
	St Bartholomew's Day massacre of 2,000–3,000 Hugenots in France
1574	Catholic priests are sent to England from France to re-establish Catholicism
1576	Demands in Parliament for greater freedom of speech
	Archbishop Grindal rejects Elizabeth's orders to suppress Puritans. Grindal is suspended
1577	William of Orange made Head of State of the United Provinces – leads resistance against Spanish rule
1578	Spain sends the Duke of Parma to pacify the Netherlands
	Mary Queen of Scots's son assumes power as King James VI of Scotland
1579	Southern provinces of the Netherlands make peace with Spain
	Marriage negotiations take place between Elizabeth and the Duke of Alençon
1577–80	Sir Francis Drake successfully circumnavigates the world
1580	Philip II of Spain inherits the crown of Portugal
	First Jesuit missions arrive in England in secrecy
1582	Marriage negotiations with the Duke of Alençon broken off
1579–83	Rebellion in Ireland
1583	Throckmorton Plot to depose Elizabeth with foreign assistance

1584	Treaty of Joinville – Spain and France form united Catholic front against England
	Assassination of William of Orange, Protestant resistance leader in the Spanish Netherlands
	Death of the Duke of Alençon
1585	Foundation of first English colony in Virginia
	Spanish troops succeed against Dutch rebels who are in revolt against Spanish rule. Elizabeth sends Earl of Leicester with military aid to the rebels
1585–1604	War with Spain
1586	Babington Plot – attempt to assassinate Elizabeth and replace her with Mary Queen of Scots
1586–7	Puritans lead Parliamentary attack on the office of bishops
1587	Execution of Mary Queen of Scots for involvement in plots against Elizabeth
	Sir Francis Drake attacks the assembling Spanish Armada at Cadiz
1588	Spanish Armada fails in its attempt to invade England
1593	Rebellion breaks out in Ireland
1596	Second Spanish Armada sent against England fails
1596–7	Poor harvests cause widespread distress
1598	An Act for the Relief of the Poor
	An Act for the Punishment of Rogues, Vagabonds and sturdy Beggars
1599	The Earl of Essex's expedition to suppress the Irish Rebellion fails
1601	Essex's rebellion to depose Elizabeth
1603	Elizabeth dies, ending the Tudor dynasty
	Accession of the Stuart king, James VI of Scotland to the English throne as James I
	Defeat of the Irish Rebellion

In the beginning

Elizabeth's childhood seems to have left on her character an indelible print which influenced her actions and attitudes as Queen. When she was two years old, in 1536, her mother Anne Boleyn was charged with treason and beheaded on the orders of Elizabeth's father, Henry VIII (see Figure 1). Many people, both in England and abroad, regarded Henry's marriage to Anne as invalid, a convenience which had enabled him to get rid of his first wife, Catherine of Aragon, who had produced only a daughter and stillborn children. On her mother's execution, Elizabeth was duly declared illegitimate and barred from the succession, although she was later restored on the accession of her half-brother Edward VI in 1547. Henry's divorce from Catherine might have caused only a minor ripple if it had not brought with it a quarrel with the Church of Rome over its refusal to nullify the marriage. As a consequence, Henry declared the Pope no longer held jurisdiction over the church in England and assumed the position of Supreme Head himself.

This left Elizabeth in an extremely vulnerable position. When her father died in 1547, his only son Edward became King. Edward VI was a staunch Protestant so Elizabeth was physically safe. But despite her restoration to the succession she was still regarded by many as the bastard offspring of an illegal marriage. And Edward's death in 1553 put her in even greater peril.

Fortunately for her survival, she was highly intelligent and well-educated. She was taught by some of the greatest scholars of the time, including Roger Ascham, a gifted teacher. She learnt Latin and Greek, was fluent in French and Italian and was well versed in the intricacies of the religious debates of the age. Added to her academic accomplishments were athleticism and musical skill. She had also been forced from an early age to understand and play by the harsh rules and realities of political life.

On her father's death, Elizabeth was sent to live with the King's widow, Katherine Parr, and it was here that the Lord Protector's younger brother, raised to the position of Lord High Admiral by his brother, began to press his suit for Katherine's hand in marriage. They were secretly married, and after the Lord Protector, Thomas Seymour had feigned offence at their not seeking his approval, the younger Seymour moved into the household. Elizabeth was enchanted by him and soon developed an adolescent crush on the Admiral. Seymour exercised little discretion in his playfulness with Elizabeth and if he found her still in bed, 'he would put open the curtains and ... make as though he would come at her ... One morning he straved to have kissed her in her bed'. Elizabeth had sufficient presence of mind to keep Seymour's attentions at a distance but the situation was rapidly becoming potentially scandalous. Elizabeth was moved to the household of Sir Anthony Denny and his wife at Cheshunt in Hertfordshire, and although annoyed at first, began to see the incident in a more mature light. It was a lesson she learnt well – that it was necessary to avoid being implicated in any scandal.

Elizabeth required all her skills not only later as Queen but, more immediately, to survive the reign of Mary I, who set about restoring the Catholic Church to England. Mary regarded Elizabeth as the cause of Henry VIII's divorce from her mother, Catherine of Aragon. Her loathing for her half-sister and their positions on opposite sides of the religious fence left Elizabeth in a dangerous position as a potential rallying point for Protestants. Initially, Elizabeth attempted to conciliate Mary by ascribing her own religious affiliations to her defective upbringing, but when Mary put Elizabeth's conversion to the test, the young princess attempted every delaying device she could think of. Their relationship became so strained that Elizabeth requested permission to retire to the country. Opposition to Mary's marriage to Philip of Spain coalesced into a conspiracy to displace the Queen and to offer the crown to Elizabeth. It is uncertain how much Elizabeth knew of the plans but, once the plot was uncovered, it confirmed in Mary's mind that Elizabeth would always represent a focal point of opposition to her. Mary was all too aware of the possibility of plots against her and on one occasion Elizabeth was imprisoned in the Tower of London for alleged complicity in Wyatt's Rebellion (1554). By a combination of guile and discretion, Elizabeth survived and on Mary's death in 1558 became Queen at the age of 25, her political skills honed to a fine art.

The 'making' of Elizabeth

The 'image-making' of Elizabeth began as soon as she became Queen, largely inspired by **Protestants** who cast her in the role of a saviour, who had rescued them from 'Bloody' Mary and the Catholic Church. This image was fostered by books such as John Foxe's *Acts and Monuments* (1563) in which Elizabeth was portrayed as protected by God in order that she might restore the true religion and suppress the Antichrist of Roman Catholicism.

KEY TERM

Protestantism originated in Germany in the early sixteenth century when a monk, Martin Luther, attacked the dogma and authority of the Roman Catholic Church. For Luther and the other reformers, God was omnipotent and it was only through His grace that mankind could be saved from sin. To achieve this, the believer must have faith, for doing good works was not sufficient.

Luther also challenged the authority of the Church to forgive sins; he believed forgiveness to be the sole province of God and the sinner. The sale of indulgences to raise money for the Church helped to crystallise Luther's opposition.

Lastly, Luther attacked the dogma of the Roman Catholic Church, particularly its emphasis on the presence of God in the host during mass – the belief known as transubstantiation.

Other Protestant leaders emerged, amongst whom Calvin in Geneva promoted a theocracy of Church elders. This brand of Protestantism took root in Scotland, whereas in England Henry VIII declared the Pope's authority at an end and that of the monarch to be supreme in the Church of England.

Popular literature and ballads peddled the same idea – Elizabeth's divine right to rule:

◢ Source 1

All English hearts rejoice and sing
That fears the Lord and loves our Queen;
Yield thanks to God, our heavenly king,
Who hitherto her guide hath been.

A Godly ditty to be sung for the preservation of the Queen's most excellent majesty's reign *(1586); quoted in C. Haigh (ed.),* **The Reign of Elizabeth I** *(Macmillan, 1984)*

Her official welcome into Warwick in 1572 listed her virtues:

⌁ Source 2

… the great benefits received from God by the happy and long-desired entrance of your Majesty into the imperial throne of this realm, after the pitiful slaughter and exile of many of your Highness' godly subjects, the restoration of the true religion, the speedy change of wars into peace, of dearth and famine into plenty, of a huge mass of dross and counterfeit money into gold and silver, to your Highness' great honour.

*Quoted in I. Dawson, **The Tudor Century 1485–1603** (Nelson, 1993)*

Elizabeth's accession, 17 November, became an official celebration. When it became evident in the 1570s that Elizabeth would not marry, the hero worship took on another more powerful aspect. Elizabeth now became a Madonna, the virgin queen, wedded to her country. Portraits began to include symbolical and allegorical detail and they represented Elizabeth as 'forever young'. In poetry she was likened to the Roman poet Virgil's Astraea, the just virgin who overcame superstition and ignorance to bring about everlasting peace. This image seems to have outweighed popular rumours of her loose morals earlier in her reign, including one that she had borne a baby to Robert Dudley. Not until the 1590s did the hostile mutterings return:

⌁ Source 3

The Queen is but woman and ruled by noblemen, and the noblemen and gentlemen are all one, and the gentlemen and farmers will hold together so that the poor can get nothing … we shall never have a merry world while the Queen liveth.

*Reported conversation of an Essex labourer, (1591); quoted in I. Dawson, **The Tudor Century 1485–1603** (Nelson, 1993)*

As the 1590s went on, the propaganda went into overdrive. In Thomas Dekker's play of 1599, *Old Fortunatus*, Dekker describes a pilgrimage made to the temple of Eliza:

◢ Source 4

Even to the temple are my feeble limbs travelling. Some call her Pandora, some Gloriana, some Cynthia, some Belphoebe, some Astraea, all by several names to express several loves. Yet all those names make but one celestial body, as all those loves meet to create but one soul ... Blessed name, happy country; your Eliza makes your land Elysium.

Thomas Dekker, **Old Fortunatus** *(1599)*

Elizabeth had been transformed into a goddess.

What's in a picture?

The manipulation of Elizabeth's image extended to her portraiture. Her concern for how she wished to be represented reveals much about her temperament and personality.

Princess Elizabeth aged about 13.

1575 – Painted by Federigo Zuccaro. This portrait was used as a template for all official portraits until the 1590s: pinholes were made outlining her main features. The template was then laid on a fresh canvas and dusted over with chalk. Further copies could then be made from the tracing.

1580–3 – The 'sieve' portrait. The sieve was a symbol of virginity which dated from Roman times. Close to Elizabeth, a globe represents England's perceived role as the founder of an overseas empire.

1592 – The 'Ditchley' portrait by Marcus Gheerarts. Here, Elizabeth is seen astride England. Storms are banished and sunshine filters through the clouds. Claims of divine intervention, such as the storm that scattered and destroyed much of the Spanish Armada of 1588, were often made by the Protestant cause.

1592 – Isaac Oliver's portrait was intended as a new template but only one copy has been found and it is unlikely that further copies were made.

The judgement of historians

KEY TERM

Historiography – Historians, as much as everyone else, are influenced by the events they live through. The study of the way in which these contemporary factors affect historical interpretation is called **historiography**. It is important to remember that whilst historians may consciously see parallels between past and present events or may be influenced unconsciously by these same factors, their historical interpretation may not necessarily be wrong, providing that there is substantial and convincing evidence to support the judgements they reach.

The first account of Elizabeth's reign was written in the 1620s by William Camden. His praise for Elizabeth was unqualified and unrestrained. He described her reign as:

◢ Source 5

The all glorious, all-virtuous, incomparable, invict and matchless pattern of princes, the glory, honour and mirror of womankind, the admiration of our age, Elizabeth, Queen of England, was by the father's side truly royal ... No oblivion shall ever bury the glory of her name, for her happy and renowned memory shall live forever in the minds of men to all prosperity, as of one who (to use no other than her successor's expression) in wisdom and felicity of government surpassed (without envy be it spoken) all the princes since the days of Augustus.

W. Camden, **Annales: The True and Royall History of the famous Empresse Elizabeth, Queen of England France and Ireland, etc. True Faith's Defendresse, of Divine Renowne and Happy Memory** (1625)

Camden was undoubtedly proud of his country and probably moved to record this ecstatic portrait by a number of factors. He was born in 1551 and began to research his subject under the influence of Elizabeth's Secretary of State Lord Burghley. He laid the project aside in 1598 after two years' endeavour, only to take it up again in 1608 under pressure from James I to provide a re-evaluation of James's mother, Mary Queen of Scots. Indeed, Mary emerged from his history as a misunderstood and misled monarch, whose execution had been agreed to by Elizabeth only under duress. Inevitably, James emerged as the champion of just causes:

◢ Source 6

[James had] laboured all that he possibly could ... to save her life, and omitted nothing that became a most dutiful and pious son ... the King of Scots, her only son, who respected his mother with the greatest piety that could be found or imagined in a son, took exceeding great hearty grief mixed with deep pleasure at the same, and very much lamented and mourned for her.

W. Camden, ***Annales: The True and Royall History of the famous Empresse Elizabeth, Queen of England France and Ireland, etc. True Faith's Defendresse, of Divine Renowne and Happy Memory*** *(1625)*

Camden was writing his history at a time of general disillusionment with James's government. In hindsight, it appeared that England's triumphs under Elizabeth outshone those of James and whilst this could not be stated explicitly in Camden's history, it was implied.

Camden's version of events exerted considerable influence on subsequent interpretations. Sir Robert Naunton, born in 1563, entered government service in 1596 and held high office from 1618. Despite his position, he was a frequent critic of government policy, which led to his suspension from the Privy Council in 1630 and his dismissal in 1635. Thereafter, he began writing about Elizabeth and her courtiers, his version of events heavily underscored by his anti-Catholic and anti-Spanish feeling. His fragmentary notes were published by his friends in 1641 when England was embroiled in the arguments between King and Parliament that were soon to lead to the Civil War.

◢ Source 7

... she ruled much by faction and parties, which herself both made, upheld and weakened, as her own great judgement advised, for I disassent from the common received opinion that my lord of Leicester was absolute and above all in her grace.

Sir Robert Naunton, ***Fragmenta Regalia*** *(London, 1641); quoted in S. H. P. Holmes, **Elizabethan England** (McDougall, 1977)*

The contrast with the Stuart king, Charles I was clear for any perceptive follower of events. Elizabeth was portrayed as running a broad-based government, playing one faction off against another. Charles, by implication and contrast, appeared weak and firmly under the control of favourites, so leading England to the brink of national disunity and destruction. Elizabeth was also portrayed as the friend of Parliament and the Protestant champion.

Neither of these conclusions can be supported by the actual events of Elizabeth's reign. Camden and Naunton were more concerned to use the image of Elizabeth for political and moral messages – Camden to show James how a great monarch should behave and Naunton to demonstrate the cause of Protestantism and the blessings of Parliamentary harmony.

This glowing portrait remained virtually intact for several centuries, apart from occasional and incidental sniping. In 1874, J. R. Green produced the definitive version of Elizabeth as the shrewd political operator who knew instinctively how to wield power, through a skilful combination of persuasion and pressure to create national unity and strength. Subsequent Victorian biographers emphasised the bond between monarch and people so that Elizabeth became transformed into an expression of the will of the nation.

After minor criticisms made by the nineteenth-century historian Thomas Macaulay, Elizabeth's reputation soared to dizzying heights in the last quarter of the nineteenth century. Britain, at this time, possessed an empire which dominated almost a quarter of the world's surface and it was inevitable that the glorification of this achievement would turn people's attention to its origins in the overseas expansion which had begun in the reign of Elizabeth.

The general adulation persisted during the 1920s and 1930s under very different conditions – economic dislocation and the growing threats to democracy in several countries, including Nazi Germany. It was at this time that J. E. Neale produced his influential biography, *Queen Elizabeth I*, which made the 'best sellers' list of 1934. The work was reprinted in 1952 at the accession of Elizabeth II, hailed at the time as the dawn of a national resurgence – a second Elizabethan Age. In his subsequent works Neale continued the lavish praise, which became so unreserved that a schoolgirl was reputed to have asked him if he had fallen in love with the long-dead monarch. Elizabeth was seen as a symbol of resistance against Spanish aggression in the same way as

Britain stood alone against Hitler. After the Second World War, the romance and colour of Elizabethan court politics provided welcome escape from rationing and scarcity. One further work by Neale on the Elizabethan Age also became influential. In *The Elizabethan House of Commons* (Jonathan Cape, 1949), Neale argued that Elizabeth's Parliaments had become the battleground of competing ideologies of extreme Puritans and Catholics. Elizabeth, however, had remained untarnished in the conflict by adeptly steering a truly liberal middle course between the extremes. Perhaps he had in mind the way the post-war world was divided between communism and capitalism as the Cold War began.

◢ Source 8

Had it not been for her [Elizabeth], the broad way of English life would have been narrowed and an experiment made with what we today term the ideological state ... [This way made possible] the greatness of the Elizabethan Age.

J. E. Neale, **Elizabeth I and her Parliaments** (Jonathan Cape, 1953)

Neale's interpretation is examined further in Chapter 2. It was strongly criticised by Professor G. Elton in his book *The Tudor Constitution* (CUP, 1960) and *The Parliament of England 1559–1581* (CUP, 1986).

◢ Source 9

... Until about sixty years ago it was generally held that in the sixteenth century Parliament played very little part in the system of government which centred on an exceptionally strong, even autocratic, monarchy ... Neale believed in a marked evolutionary scheme for the history of the Tudor Parliament, a progress from underdeveloped beginnings handed on by the Middle Ages to 'maturity' under Elizabeth.

G. R. Elton, 'Parliament' in C. Haigh (ed.), **The Reign of Elizabeth I** (Macmillan, 1984)

There seems, however, no waning in the interest for Elizabeth and her reign. More than one hundred biographies have been published since 1890 and the vast majority are favourable to Elizabeth's government.

Some historians, such as Christopher Haigh, have been a little more critical, but by and large the judgement remains in favour of Elizabeth.

◢ Source 10

... the historiographical wheel has come almost full circle. A 'revisionist' argument which diminished Elizabeth's achievement by weakening the forces she is said to have controlled has apparently rehabilitated her reign as an era of concord. We are back – give or take a bread riot or two – with an Elizabethan golden age! Harmony at court, harmony in Parliament, harmony (or at least no serious disputes) in the localities, harmony in religion, harmony between social classes ... There is a risk that, in their determination to escape from a polarising and crisis-laden Civil War perspective, historians will fall into a false 'Merrie England' romanticism which explains away every problem and sees near-success in each disaster.

C. Haigh (ed.), **The Reign of Elizabeth I** (Macmillan, 1984)

The Tudor state

At her accession in 1558, Elizabeth I, in common with her predecessors, was in no doubt that she not merely reigned but ruled. Nevertheless, she was female, single, regarded by many European Catholic noblemen as the illegitimate offspring of Henry VIII's mistress, Anne Boleyn, and England was still technically at war with France. Furthermore, she had inherited a kingdom which was a second-rate power, overshadowed by Spain and France, and divided by religious confusion. It was obvious that in order to survive in such a hostile climate she would need to create and maintain a strong and effective government.

Elizabeth had to tackle these problems with an inherited system of government. To understand the nature of this government it is important to understand the social structure in which it operated and the expectations and attitudes of those who were its key players.

Elizabethan society and government

Society was seen as essentially hierarchical, ordained by God. The most significant distinction lay between those who governed and those in the lower orders who did not (the horizontal line in Figure 2). Expanding trade, however, had created a merchant class which possessed a degree of social mobility and it was possible for members of this order to graduate into the gentry by buying landed estates.

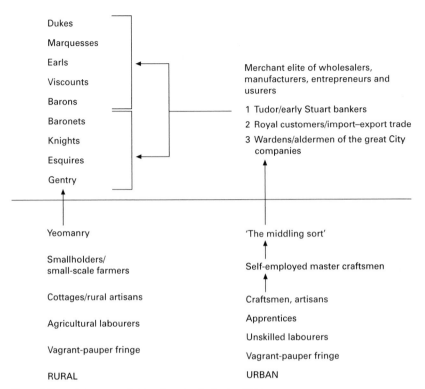

Figure 2 The social structure of sixteenth-century England and Wales
(source: M. A. R. Graves and R. H. Silcock, *Revolution, Reaction and the Triumph of Conservatism*, Longman Paul, 1984)

Possession of land was key to one's position on the social ladder as well as to the political packing order. The established Church mirrored these social hierarchies.

At the peak of the political pyramid sat the monarch (see Figure 3). Whilst the powers of the monarch were wide, they were exercised through a number of institutions which could exert a modifying influence on the ruler's actions. Nevertheless, to be close to power meant being close to the monarch, usually as a member of the Royal Court, but more significantly as a member of the policy-making **Privy Council**. Under Mary this body had become large and unwieldy and dominated by the nobility. Elizabeth formed it into a tightly-knit group of between 12 and 20, with an inner ring of less than a dozen who were effectively the policy makers. She also ensured that a wide

CROWN

- an integral part of all sections: none
  exist without crown
- has power over all sections
- chief executive
- final decision maker
- wide prerogative power
- leader
- ratifies all laws

CHURCH   **JUDICIARY**

- chief positions appointed by crown
- responsible to crown
- have 'dual' allegiance:
  • to crown
  • to profession

EXECUTIVE

1 Privy Council
  - chief administrator
  - advises crown
  - influences crown
  - responsible to crown

Secretaries
  - advise crown
  - often Councillors
  - appointed by crown
  - responsible to crown

2 Local administration
(Lords Lieutenant, Justices of the Peace, Sheriffs)
  - carry out executive decisions
  - appointed by crown
  - responsible to crown

3 Parliament
  - dependent on crown to be called or dismissed
  - does NOT run country or make decisions
  - consists of three parts:
    • The Sovereign
      - can approve/veto all legislation
    • Lords (peers, bishops, judges)
      - initiates legislation
      - approves/rejects Commons bills
      - influenced by Councillors
    • Commons (elected)
      - limited powers of debate
      - legislative function
      - votes on extra-ordinary finance
      - influenced by Councillors

Figure 3 Government of England under Elizabeth I at Elizabeth's accession

spectrum of political and religious views was represented in her Council but left Councillors in no doubt that they were entirely dependent on her wishes.

In turn, the Privy Council reached down into the apparatus of government at all levels. It appointed and supervised the local magistrates as well as staffing the **Prerogative Courts of Chancery** (dealing with wills and civil matters), the **Star Chamber** (asserting royal power in all parts and at all levels of society) and the **High Commission** (covering the governance of the Church). The key significance of all these institutions was that they derived their power from the crown's authority. There was no equivalent of a modern prime minister but the office which provided the widest overview of government business was that of **Secretary of State**. During the reign of Elizabeth's father, Henry VIII, his Secretary of State Thomas Cromwell had made this office the nerve centre of power. Appointing the Secretary of State was, therefore, a crucial decision. On the day of Elizabeth's accession she named William Cecil (see Picture Gallery), the youngest member of the Council, to this post. He was to remain in office until his death in 1598 at what was for then the impressive age of 78.

Cecil was also given the post of **Lord Treasurer**, another crucial appointment for he was in charge of the **exchequer**, the main money-gathering agency for the crown. He also held this position for 40 years and was succeeded as Lord Treasurer by his son, Robert.

The Privy Councillors were an important link between the crown and **Parliament**. They sat in both the **House of Commons** and the **House of Lords**, controlled the business of both **Houses** and initiated the legislation the monarch wished to be enacted. Parliaments were only called at the instruction of the crown to discuss specific issues initiated by the Queen. Furthermore, Parliament could be ***prorogued*** (adjourned) and dissolved when the monarch decided.

Despite the overwhelming balance of power in favour of the monarch, Parliament had increased in power and prestige during the fifteenth century and particularly during the reign of Henry VIII. This was for two reasons. Firstly, the legislation to achieve the ***Reformation*** (1529–36) in England was immense and Parliaments had been summoned with increasing regularity for this purpose. As a consequence, their authority to act together with the monarch was enhanced. Secondly, during the fifteenth century and again during Henry VIII's reign, statutes (laws made by the crown in conjunction with Parliament) carried greater weight than proclamations (issued solely by the monarch).

It was not surprising that Members of Parliament (MPs) showed little opposition both to the specific policies and to the underlying functions of government for they were essentially drawn from the ruling gentry. **Boroughs** were towns entitled by Royal Charter to run their own affairs and elect an MP but in fact most were controlled by the crown or by a local magnate. In the case of **county** members, the vast majority were clients of courtiers or of an influential local landowner.

The Privy Council sent out a constant stream of instructions on all matters to the **local administrators**. Responsibility for carrying out these instructions resided with the Queen's personal representative in every county, the **Lord Lieutenant**, who was meant to supervise those responsible for law and order. But the day-to-day task of ensuring that laws were implemented fell on the shoulders of the **Justices of the Peace** (JPs), who were nominated out of both the higher and the lower gentry. Local interests and attitudes dominated their actions and for this reason instructions from the Privy Council were not always implemented diligently.

KEY TERMS

Reformation – In the Middle Ages, the Roman Catholic Church exercised enormous power, from the Pope downwards, through cardinals and bishops to priests at the parish level. Such a massive and powerful institution inevitably attracted criticism which during the sixteenth century reached new intensity and effectiveness. A major attack was led by Martin Luther, who argued that the vast apparatus of church organisation was unnecessary to achieve salvation. Luther's ideas and those of other reformers such as Calvin in Geneva spread across northern Europe. By the end of the sixteenth century the Christian Church was deeply divided between various Protestant sects, who broke from Rome, and the Roman Catholic Church.

Prorogation – The right of the monarch to discontinue the meetings of Parliament for a time without dissolving it.

Elizabeth's reign

In this section we shall look briefly at Elizabeth's reign, dividing it into five main phases, and including some key features of each phase.

First steps to power, 1558–60

Elizabeth Tudor became queen on 17 November 1558. She was 25 years old and there was a sense of anticipation that her reign would be a fresh start. Her accession, however, was fraught with difficulties: she was female, regarded by many foreign powers as illegitimate and her country was still at war with France. North of the border in Scotland, Mary of Guise ruled as regent on behalf of her daughter, Mary Stuart, who was married to the heir of the French throne. England feared that this northern outpost could be used as a springboard from which to launch a combined invasion.

Peace with France

Elizabeth needed to end as many of these uncertainties as she could. In 1559 the **Treaty of Cateau-Cambrésis** was signed with France. It did not return Calais, England's last remnant of its French empire lost to France in Mary's reign, to England, but there was a promise of financial compensation. To have remained at war would anyway have been immeasurably worse.

Scotland

In Scotland Protestantism had taken root and the French Catholic regent, Mary of Guise, had provoked Scottish noblemen into revolt. Cecil urged intervention on their behalf and, after initial hesitation, Elizabeth agreed to send an expeditionary force. Mary of Guise died soon after and French troops capitulated, withdrawing from the country following the terms of the **Treaty of Edinburgh** of 1560.

The need for a religious settlement

Elizabeth's most pressing domestic problem was the need for a religious settlement after 25 years of dramatic change. Henry VIII had made the break with Rome by declaring himself, not the Pope, as head of the Church of England but he had made no other real doctrinal changes in religion. A significant shift to Protestant forms of worship had taken place during the reign of Henry's son, Edward VI. Mary Tudor had attempted to reverse the tide of Protestantism by reinstating the authority of the Pope and the liturgy of Catholicism. Elizabeth had been brought up as a Protestant, so a settlement along Protestant lines was widely expected. By the **Act of Supremacy** of 10 April 1559, the English monarch became the **Supreme Governor** of the Church of England. In order to define forms of worship and, in particular, to adopt the Book of Common Prayer, the **Act of Uniformity** of 18 April 1559 quickly followed.

Marriage and the succession

Elizabeth was one of the best prizes in Europe from a matrimonial standpoint, despite England's empty treasury. From the outset of her reign, a host of domestic and foreign suitors courted Elizabeth. The Earl of Arundel and Sir William Pickering were rumoured to have hopes of marriage, while Philip II of Spain and Prince Eric of Sweden, both sons of the Holy Roman Emperor, actually proposed marriage. The Spanish ambassador reported that the court was swarming with offers from many more. Even Parliament pressed the Queen to marry to ensure that the succession of the crown was not disturbed by claim and counter-claim. Elizabeth responded to this last request: 'I will never in that matter conclude anything that shall be prejudicial to the realm … And in the end this shall be for me sufficient, that a marble stone shall declare that a Queen having reigned such a time, lived and died a virgin.'

In 1560 Archduke Charles of Austria appeared to be the favourite prospect but gossip of an affair between Dudley and the Queen cancelled out any interest. The suspicious death of Dudley's wife in September 1560 put paid to any advancement of this affair. Meanwhile, negotiations continued with the Swedish ambassador.

Elizabeth's near death from smallpox in 1562 accelerated the discussion of marriage and succession. The Parliament of 1563 implored 'that it please your Majesty to dispose yourself to marry, where you will, and with whom you will, and as shortly as you will'. The MPs' motivation for making this appeal was to avoid the disorder that a disputed succession would provoke. Elizabeth, as she did so often, prevaricated by saying that she had not vowed to stay unmarried and that she would settle the succession when the time was right. This uncertainty provided considerable opportunity for any number of cliques to press their claim, frequently through Parliament. Elizabeth became irritated at the constant demands and told them 'it is monstrous that the feet should direct the head'.

By the early 1570s Elizabeth was increasingly determined to retain her freedom of action. Nevertheless, she encouraged the suits of the dukes of Anjou and Alençon, but it became apparent that this was a smokescreen behind which she could deny that she had resolved to remain the almost beatified virgin queen.

Consolidating power, 1560–6
Currency reform
An important early priority for Elizabeth's government was to place England's currency on a secure footing. Successive debasements of the **coinage** had taken place during the reigns of successive Tudor monarchs, to the extent that coins contained such high percentages of alloys that they were worth less than their face value. English merchants abroad found themselves unable to trade, except in gold. This in turn caused a drain on gold from England. Under Cecil's guiding hand nearly £670,000 in debased coins were returned to the mint and refined, allowing Elizabeth to claim that she had achieved 'the victory and conquests of this hideous monster of the base moneys'.

Protestantism in Scotland ...
The running sore of England's relationship with France and Scotland continued to weep. Mary Queen of Scots had returned to Scotland from France after the premature death of her husband in December 1560, provoking new fears of French intervention, particularly as many Catholics, including the King of France, regarded Mary as the rightful Queen of England too. However, Mary's power in her newly inherited kingdom was not secure. *Calvinism* all but dominated the country, thus isolating the Catholic monarch. To counteract French influence Mary was persuaded to marry an English-educated but Scottish nobleman, **Lord Darnley**, with disastrous consequences.

Key Term

Calvinism was the term used for those Protestants who followed the teaching of John Calvin, a Protestant reformer in the Swiss city of Geneva in the 1540s. The Calvinist Church was one of stark simplicity in furniture and service with strict regulation of the behaviour of the congregation. At the heart of Calvin's beliefs was the theory of **predestination**, i.e. that some individuals were 'saved' whilst others were damned and that these fates had been predetermined. Needless to say, it was those who followed the strict Calvinist code who were likely to be saved. At the same time Calvin placed great emphasis on each individual seeking his own salvation. Elizabeth disliked the implied irrelevance of Church hierarchies in this belief. Calvin had considerable influence on Protestants in England and particularly in Scotland.

... and in France

If England feared the reassertion of French influence in Scotland, France itself was preoccupied with internal problems. French Protestants, known as **Huguenots**, had made significant gains, focusing power in strong centres such as La Rochelle. The religious divisions were becoming so acute that civil war threatened the stability of the country. Elizabeth did not want to get involved too deeply in this conflict but agreed to send an expeditionary force to aid the Huguenots in September 1562. The military position for the Huguenots worsened and by 10 March 1563 a settlement had been reached with the French crown.

Threats to the state, 1566–72

Mary Queen of Scots

On 10 February 1567, Lord Darnley, Mary Queen of Scots' husband, was blown up. The Queen and her friend Lord Bothwell, who later became her third husband, were deeply implicated in the death. After a series of skirmishes and a period of imprisonment, Mary fled across the border to England in 1568, expecting help from Elizabeth to regain her kingdom. This began a twenty-year-long imprisonment in England for Mary. Elizabeth kept her under arrest as she dared not let Mary, a possible rival to her throne, fall into enemy hands. Mary became the focus of several plots against Elizabeth but Elizabeth still could not bring herself to dispose of her troublesome captive.

The Netherlands

The problem of the future of Mary Queen of Scots became entangled with relationships with Spain. The **Netherlands** was crucial to England's single most important trading staple – wool. This loose collection of provinces was part of the territory of the Spanish crown and if trouble arose there it would put English trade in jeopardy. In the early sixteenth century, the Netherlands was swept by Calvinism. The King of Spain, Philip II, despatched the Duke of Alba to restore religious uniformity in 1566. By 1568 the Netherlands had been subjugated but discontent rumbled on and Elizabeth was under pressure to become involved. After England seized Spanish treasure from the America fleets, Spain retaliated by confiscating English goods in the Netherlands. Philip turned his attention to a possible invasion of England in which Elizabeth would be deposed and replaced by Mary.

Threats to Elizabeth, at home and abroad

The Duke of Norfolk saw an opportunity to marry Mary and thus inherit the English crown. To further his aims he made contact with the Spanish ambassador and began to plot the assassination of Elizabeth. Meanwhile, the earls of Cumberland and Westmorland fomented rebellion in the north on behalf of Norfolk. **The Northern Rising** began in 1569 with the aim of removing Elizabeth and restoring the old religion. But the revolt fizzled out and the earls were executed. Amazingly, Norfolk escaped direct implication.

Mary Queen of Scots was moved further south and her conditions of captivity tightened. Elizabeth gave instructions for a death warrant to be drawn up but she was reluctant to be responsible for the execution of an ordained monarch. In 1570, Lord Moray, the regent of Scotland during the infancy of James IV, was assassinated, rekindling fears that Scottish nobles would insist on the return of Mary Queen of Scots and with her, worst of all, French influence. Elizabeth played for time with the French over the restoration of Mary. Then, on 25 February 1570, Pope Pius V formally *excommunicated* Elizabeth.

KEY TERM

Excommunication – This was a serious assault on the legitimacy of Elizabeth's reign. Technically, to the Catholics, excommunication placed Elizabeth outside the Church and released her legitimate subjects from loyalty to the crown – in short, any subject could now engage in rebellion against the Queen. English Catholics were in a dilemma – should their loyalty be to the Pope or to the Queen? Most, however, remained quiescent.

In April 1571 Parliament extended the definition of treason, which made the situation for Catholics extremely hazardous. In this tense atmosphere a further plot was discovered – **the Ridolfi Plot**, named after a Florentine banker, who secretly negotiated with Mary Queen of Scots and the Duke of Norfolk for an invasion of England from the Netherlands. This time, Norfolk did not escape punishment for his complicity and in 1572 he was executed. Again, Elizabeth's Councillors pressed for the death of Mary but the most she would concede through a Parliamentary act was the debarring of the Scots Queen from the English succession.

Relations with France

In the face of Spanish aggression, Elizabeth sought alliance with France. This was cemented in 1572 by the **Treaty of Blois**. The new alliance, however, was put in jeopardy with the massacre of some 2,000–3,000 French Protestants on **St Bartholomew's Day**, 24 August 1572. In this circumstance, Elizabeth began to assist the Huguenots but did so discreetly so as to avoid huge financial commitments. Meanwhile, fear of French influence in Scotland ended with the ascendancy of the Protestant Scottish nobles, who captured Edinburgh Castle in 1573 from Mary's supporters.

Elizabeth triumphant, 1572–88

Intervention in the Netherlands

Matters in the Netherlands dominated England's foreign policy. The Duke of Alba was keen to lift the embargo on English trade, feeling that prosperity was the most effective method in the long-term aim of restoring Spain's suzerainty. The **Treaty of Bristol**, concluded between the two powers in 1574, ended the embargo on English trade in return for the withdrawal of support for the rebels. The religious war in the Netherlands dragged on, with Elizabeth giving only occasional, and sparing, support to the rebels. In 1584 **William of Orange** was assassinated and by 1585 it was evident that Dutch resistance would be at an end without English assistance. Under the terms of the **Treaty of Nonsuch**, 1585, the Earl of Leicester took command of an English expeditionary force sent to the aid of the Netherlands. He proved ineffective but events nearer home were becoming more problematic and Leicester was recalled for a crucial decision.

The Spanish Armada, 1588

In 1586 the **Babington Plot** was exposed. Mary's complicity in a conspiracy to murder Elizabeth and encourage a Spanish invasion was revealed. Elizabeth needed support at this most difficult time for it was impossible now to evade a decision on the fate of Mary Queen of Scots. To a man, her Councillors urged execution but still Elizabeth was reluctant to take the final step. After further prevarication she gave the order and Mary was beheaded on 8 February 1587.

Catholic Europe was appalled at the death of the Scots Queen and Philip of Spain, with the Pope's blessing, appointed himself the instrument of revenge, although he had many other reasons for wanting to deal with Elizabeth. His plan to launch a seaborne invasion of England by uniting with Spanish troops in the Netherlands, however, was defeated in 1588. All further invasion attempts failed.

English Catholics and Protestants

The anticipated rebelliousness of Elizabeth's Catholic subjects never came to pass, largely as a result of Elizabeth's reluctance to make life difficult for them, although she did allow Parliament to increase penalties on Catholics. Parliament was much more concerned and tightened legislation, increasing penalties on Catholics in 1591.

Meanwhile, there was agitation at the other end of the religious spectrum. Some Protestants, particularly the **Puritans**, were dissatisfied with the Religious Settlement of 1559 and wished for further reforms to the Church of England.

KEY TERM

Puritan is a term used to describe those members of the Church of England who called themselves 'godly'. The 'godly' believed that the Protestant reform of the Church should be carried much further. They were intensely hostile to any practice or ritual which so much as hinted at Roman Catholicism. They wanted to remove the office of bishops and to transform people's spiritual lives. By the seventeenth century, they were also targeting social behaviour.

Although the term Puritan was frequently applied to the Protestant dissenters, it would be a mistake to see them as an organised group. What they all had in common, however, was a desire to see the Church remove remaining symbols of Catholicism. Whilst many were sceptical of the office of bishops (episcopacy) they were content to accept their continued existence, as long as the bishops were 'godly'. Only committed Presbyterians were opposed to episcopacy in principle. Elizabeth saw such proposals as a challenge to her authority and the delicate Religious Settlement she felt she had achieved in 1559. Reforms were sought by Puritans in the Parliaments of 1571, 1573 and 1576, often supported by those at the heart of Elizabeth's government. Archbishop Grindal attempted to provide a compromise solution but refused to forbid the discussion groups or **prophesyings** which Elizabeth regarded as provocative. Elizabeth suspended Grindal and after the archbishop's death, appointed Whitgift, a leading opponent of the Puritan movement, as Archbishop of Canterbury.

The declining years, 1588–1603

Foreign relations

In 1588 Elizabeth appeared to be at the zenith of her powers. Although the war with Spain continued until the end of her reign, Philip had effectively been defeated and Spain's power was beginning to wane. In France, the Protestant Henry of Navarre had become King and had immediately become embroiled in a war against his own Catholic subjects who were supported by Spain in a coalition called the **Catholic League**. Thus both her powerful enemies were preoccupied. When Henry became secure on his throne in 1595 he supported Elizabeth's intervention in the Netherlands. Ideally, Elizabeth wanted neither Spain nor France to be the dominant power in the Netherlands for this would be prejudicial to England's interests. The recognition of the independence of the United Provinces of the north as Holland and the continued domination of the southern provinces by Spain as a buffer with France was exactly the settlement Elizabeth wanted.

Treatment of the poor

These wars had proved extremely costly. Inflation became rampant and was fuelled by an increased population. **The Poor Laws of 1598 and 1601** attempted to distinguish between the deserving and undeserving poor, imposing harsh penalties on vagrants.

Monopolies

Elizabeth was now obliged to turn her back on her earlier financial prudence by selling crown lands, debasing the coinage and insisting on forced loans, for although Parliaments granted triple and quadruple subsidies, there was never sufficient money to discharge the crown's obligations. Bribery increased as more people competed for a finite number of government positions. Above all, Elizabeth's practice of granting *monopolies* to raise cash drew the greatest criticism. Some monopolies were justified; others were more tenuous, for example Walter Raleigh had the monopoly on playing cards. The inevitable consequence of this practice was the raising of prices still further in a period of rapid inflation. The Parliaments of 1597 and 1601 attacked the practice and some of the worst abuses were abolished.

KEY TERM

Monopoly – The exclusive ownership or right to control a commodity through legal privilege.

Ireland

Not for the last time, events in Ireland provided problems for the English government. England had always had, at best, an insecure hold on the country, usually limited to the area around Dublin. Furthermore, the cost of governing Ireland far outweighed the miserable revenue England received in return. But England could not quit the country, fearing that it could be used as a base for invasion by an unfriendly foreign power. In 1593, an uprising broke out in Ulster, escalating into a widespread rebellion when the Earl of Tyrone became its leader in 1595. English control collapsed. In order to restore the

Queen's authority, the Earl of Essex, Leicester's step-son, was dispatched at the head of an impressive army. Desertions, disease and the ineptitude of Essex whittled away his force. The Earl deserted his troops and returned to England without the Queen's permission. Elizabeth was furious and after further misjudgements on the part of Essex, he hatched a poorly organised rebellion to depose the Queen, which failed. On 25 February 1601 he was executed. In Ireland, Lord Mountjoy was placed in command of the English army and brought Tyrone's rebellion to an end.

The last days

Whilst Elizabeth appeared to be as energetic as ever despite her advanced age she confessed that she did not possess the same will to rule as before. In February 1603 she fell into a deep depression from which she could not be roused. On 24 March 1603 she died.

TASKS

1 Key events

Look back at the timeline on pages 6–7. Cut a photocopy of the page horizontally into strips for each event. Arrange the strips into different categories of your choice.

What *types* of problems did Elizabeth face?

Don't worry too much at this stage if you don't understand fully the nature and significance of each event. Remember: a timeline is selective. As you read on, consider which other events might be added to it.

2 Elizabeth's image

Re-read the written sources relating to Elizabeth's image and look at the portraits on pages 12–13.

a For what possible reasons were these tributes made?
b What do you notice about the way the tributes change over time?
c How did Elizabeth wish to be portrayed in public?
d What do the portraits tell us about Elizabeth's concern for the way she wished to be represented?
e In what ways does Elizabeth's image change over time and why?

3 The historians' view

a In what ways might historians have been influenced in their judgements by the times in which they lived?
b Which of the historians appear to have been more aware that they were writing under the influence of contemporary events?
c If the interpretations of Elizabeth have come 'full circle', why might it be argued that the process has still been worthwhile?

King PHILIP II of Spain,
1556–98

Philip was the son of Charles I of Spain (Holy Roman Emperor Charles V). He was invested by his father with the rule of Milan, Naples, Sicily (1556–98) and of Portugal (1580–98). Philip defeated the combined forces of the Papacy and France in 1556 and by the Treaty of Cateau-Cambrésis in 1559, Spanish overlordship of the Franche-Comté and the Italian states was acknowledged. Marriage was strictly a political matter. In 1543 he married Maria, daughter of John III of Portugal, but she died in 1545. His second marriage was to Mary of England (1554–8) whom he assisted in returning the country to the Catholic Church. The marriage produced no children. His offer to marry Mary's sister, Elizabeth, was rejected, and in 1559 he married Elizabeth, daughter of Henry II of France instead. She died in 1568 and his last wife was Anne, daughter of Emperor Maximillian II.

The great objective of Philip's policy was to stem the tide of advancing Protestantism and to re-impose Catholicism where it had been expelled and to impose a uniform government throughout his realms. These aims came into conflict in the provinces of the Netherlands, where a revolt broke out in 1567. The Duke of Alba was sent to suppress the revolt but the causes were deeply embedded in all sections of Dutch society.

The Dutch provinces declared their independence in 1581 and maintained it until officially recognised in 1648 at the end of the religious wars that racked much of Europe. The southern Netherland provinces, predominantly Catholic, became reconciled to Spanish rule.

Philip attempted to form a holy alliance with France to prevent Henry of Navarre becoming King of France, but failed. He also attempted to avenge the execution of Mary Queen of Scots by launching a vast Armada against England, but this too failed. This event marked the beginning of the passing of Spanish seapower in favour of that of England.

MARY Queen of Scots,
1542–87

The story of Mary's life contains all the elements of a romantic drama – love, murder, imprisonment and escape – and legends have gathered around her personality. Mary was born a week before her father, James V of Scotland, died at the age of 30. The 'auld alliance' with France determined the diplomatic strategy of Scotland and, consequently, marriage arrangements. In 1548, Mary was sent to France, promised in marriage to the Dauphin (heir to the French crown) whilst her mother, Mary of Guise, remained in Scotland as regent and attempted to stem the tide of rising Protestantism. In 1558, Mary married the Dauphin with great pomp at the Cathedral of Notre-Dame in Paris but was widowed within two years when her husband, Francis II, who had succeeded his father in 1559, died of tuberculosis.

Meanwhile, Mary's mother had died in Scotland and so, in 1561, Mary returned to the country of which she had little memory. She entered into a disastrous marriage with Lord Darnley, an English nobleman and cousin of Queen Elizabeth. After their marriage broke down, Darnley was murdered and Mary married the chief suspect, Lord Bothwell, a Scottish nobleman. Defeated by an army raised by dissident nobles in 1567, Mary was imprisoned but escaped and fled to England in 1568, expecting that Elizabeth would restore her to her throne. The Queen of England was only too aware, however, that Mary had a claim on the English throne as the legitimate Catholic monarch. Elizabeth had her imprisoned and as Mary increasingly became a focus for Catholic plots eventually, and reluctantly, had her executed on 7 February 1587.

Sir WILLIAM CECIL, Lord Burghley, *1520–98*

William Cecil was born in 1520 and educated at Grantham Grammar School and Cambridge University. His second wife, Mildred, daughter of Sir Anthony Cooke, Prince Edward's governor, gave William an influence at court. During Edward's reign, Cecil was identified as a promising talent and promoted to the Privy Council. He fell from favour during the reign of Mary Tudor although he managed to convince the Queen of his loyalty. He never served in Mary's government so came to office under Elizabeth relatively untainted.

He was immediately made Secretary to the Privy Council, in effect First Minister, when Elizabeth became Queen. In 1561, Cecil was appointed Master of Court of Wards, an office which took responsibility for the estates of minors, and consequently a very lucrative position for both himself and the crown. Virtually all his life was devoted to Elizabeth's service, and he carried out his duties skilfully so that Elizabeth came to rely upon his tact and diplomacy. In contrast to Robert Dudley, Cecil encouraged Elizabeth to avoid foreign entanglements as a drain on the country's resources, and despite being a convinced Protestant, always put England's interests above all others, even his religion. Only once in his career did Elizabeth show him any displeasure and that was after the execution of Mary Queen of Scots. Although he had done no more than carry out her wishes it suited her to have it believed that he had misinterpreted her instructions.

In such a powerful position he acquired both the title of Lord Burghley and wealth which he spent lavishly.

Lord ROBERT DUDLEY, Earl of Leicester, *1532–88*

For many years Robert Dudley was Queen Elizabeth's favourite. He was named Master of the Horse in January 1558 and four months later sworn in as a member of the Privy Council. Dudley received many estates and gifts from the Queen as tokens of her affection and there is little doubt that she contemplated marrying him. The death of his wife, Amy Robsart, in suspicious circumstances put an end to that for all time. After a discreet absence from court he returned to royal favour. Whilst the Queen held him in regard many considered him duplicitous and he made a number of concerted attempts to have Cecil removed and even executed.

Dudley figures as the leading apologist of the Puritans at court and was in the forefront of advocating support for Protestant causes abroad. In September 1585 he was appointed Commander-in-Chief of the expeditionary force to the Low Countries to fight on behalf of the Dutch against the Spanish. His reception was overwhelming and the Dutch installed him as supreme governor although he appeared to be reluctant to take the field against the Spanish.

Elizabeth was indignant that he had accepted the title without her permission and his overbearing attitude towards the Dutch soon lost him his initial advantage with them. After a lacklustre campaign, Leicester returned home, leaving his army without command. Nevertheless, the Queen accepted him once more into her circles and he was present with the army at Tilbury in 1588 at the time of the Armada. Shortly afterwards he was taken ill and died.

PART TWO

CHAPTER ONE

HOW SUCCESSFUL WAS THE RELIGIOUS SETTLEMENT OF 1559?

Objectives
◢ To investigate the nature of the Religious Settlement of 1559
◢ To evaluate the challenges to that Settlement
◢ To determine the effectiveness of the Religious Settlement.

How was the Religious Settlement of 1559 reached?

Elizabeth's intention on coming to the throne was to find a suitable religious settlement that the broad mass of English people would accept. It was likely to be a Protestant settlement; on a personal level, because she had been brought up as a Protestant, and, politically, because she could see immense advantages in being head of the Church. Quite what the settlement would look like was not going to be easy to define. Cecil and Dudley, in common with many of the other Councillors, were convinced Protestants, but Elizabeth also quite intentionally retained Councillors who were deeply conservative. Her own inclination was not to push religious conformity to extremes. Provided the gentry acknowledged the establishment of the Church of England she did not wish to provoke their consciences any further and 'make windows into men's souls'. She wished to retain ceremony and ceremonial dress as well as the Church hierarchy to ensure a measure of conformity and control. In the first weeks of her reign, however, she insisted on using fewer candles in her chapel services, ordered the priest not to raise the host and had the words of the consecration spoken in English.

Matters of religion were at the heart of the state and Elizabeth was well aware that she needed to minimise the possibilities of widespread dissent and revolt. The arguments were much discussed in a document entitled **Device for the Alteration of Religion (1558)**. The anonymous author of the document warned Elizabeth not to assume that the dominance of Protestants in the south-east of the country represented the views of everyone. The author went on to say, 'better it were that they did not suffer than her highness and commonwealth should shake or be in danger' if the majority of people identified in any settlement 'a cloaked papistry or a mingle-mangle'. Many were not in sympathy with radical Protestantism and their adherence to the Catholic rites of worship was difficult to shake. What was certain, however, is that they did not want to be subject to the Pope's authority.

The recommendation was for a return to Edwardian forms of worship as soon as possible but the writer advised caution until Parliament had settled the content of the Book of Common Prayer. In the opinion of the anonymous writer, no unlicensed form of worship should be permitted and a close eye should be kept on the Marian bishops and officials. If JPs attacked the Settlement they should be replaced by younger members of the gentry. The author concluded that a middle course of moderate Protestantism would provide for the satisfaction of the majority and it was a middle course that Elizabeth was determined to steer.

This strategy was firmly enshrined in the two acts which were presented to Parliament in 1559:

◢ **The Act of Supremacy** – By means of this bill, Papal authority was to be abolished and Elizabeth was to assume the title of **Supreme Governor of the Church of England**, not **Supreme Head** as Henry had adopted. This was to appease those who thought it unfitting for a woman and a layperson to be head of the Church.

◢ **The Act of Uniformity** – whereby the 1552 Book of Common Prayer, with amendments to satisfy the conservative forces, was to be imposed in all English churches.

Elizabeth took notice of the advice in the **Device** and proceeded with great caution, as the imperial ambassador noted in March 1559:

◢ Source 1

From the very beginning of her reign she has treated all religious questions with so much caution and incredible prudence that she seems both to protect the Catholic religion and at the same time not entirely to condemn or reject the new Reformation. … In my opinion, a very prudent action, for the less she ruffles them at the beginning of her reign the more easily she will enthrall them at the end.

Count von Helffstein to Emperor Ferdinand I, 16 March 1559

Did religion matter?

The details of the religious arrangements set out in 1559 were not trivial issues. They mattered to people, as the commitment and passionate language of the following sources show:

◢ Source 2

I naturally want more than anything to die for Christ, but it is too much to hope that it will be by the executioner's hand … If God should make him [the priest] worthy of that glorious end, would he pray for her that she might obtain like happiness.

A Roman Catholic woman, circa 1580, quoted in A. Dures,
English Catholicism 1582–1642 *(Longman, 1983)*

◢ Source 3

Our Lord bishops … that swinish rabble, are pettie Antichrists, pettie popes, proud prelates, intolerable withstanders of reformation, enemies of the gospell and most covetous wretched priests …

Marprelate 'Epistle' Puritan 1588, quoted in I. Dawson,
The Tudor Century 1485–1603 *(Nelson, 1993)*

◢ Source 4

XIII.   Provided always and be it enacted that such ornaments of the Church, and of the ministers thereof shall be retained and be in use as was in the Church of England by authority of Parliament in the second year of the reign of King Edward VI …

Statutes of the Realm, *1559*

The need for a religious settlement

It was inevitable that a middle course was unlikely to satisfy either end of the religious spectrum. Mary's Catholic bishops lay in wait in the House of Lords and mangled the proposed legislation almost to the point of destruction. Elizabeth was therefore obliged to recall Parliament after Easter. When it reassembled it was without two bishops whom Elizabeth had imprisoned and some conservative peers who claimed they had been unavoidably detained on other business. The Act of Uniformity was enacted but by a majority of only three votes, with nine lords, including two Privy Councillors, opposing it.

Was this the settlement Elizabeth wanted or was she forced to compromise? This is not easy to judge for no draft bills exist and other sources of evidence are sparse. The most influential historian of the period, J. E. Neale, set the tone for the debate during the 1930s through to the 1950s. In *Elizabeth I and her Parliaments* (Jonathan Cape, 1953), Neale argues that a strong and united group of Puritans existed and they were successful in pushing Elizabeth to make a more radical settlement than she had intended. More recently, historians such as N. L. Jones (1984) suggest that the conservative elements in the clergy ensured that the Settlement retained much that was recognisably Catholic.

◢ Source 5

The stumbling block that had tripped her drive for a religious settlement was the power of the bishops and Catholic laymen in the House of Lords. The bishops were an especially difficult group to overcome because they were the official experts on religion.

N. L. Jones, 'Elizabeth's First Year' in C. Haigh (ed.),
The Reign of Elizabeth I (Macmillan, 1984)

◢ Source 6

Some historians, aware of weaknesses in Neale's explanation, have tried to demolish it entirely. Dr Jones believes that Elizabeth always intended to have an act of Uniformity as well as Supremacy, and that the Uniformity she wanted was that of the 1552 book.

All this is, in the final analysis, incapable of firm proof … It seems highly improbable that this settlement is what Elizabeth had intended. Certainly her subsequent actions suggest she had little sympathy for the 1559 Settlement … a month after the end of Parliament Elizabeth authorised a set of injunctions. They were conservative in tone. When we add this to Elizabeth's insistence on the use of a crucifix in the chapel royal and her dislike of married clergy, it becomes difficult to accept the arguments of … Jones about Elizabeth's Protestantism.

J. Loach and R. Tittler, ***The Mid-Tudor Polity c1540–1560*** (Macmillan, 1980)

The Settlement of 1559

The Act of Uniformity determined that all church services should be conducted according to the 1552 Book of Common Prayer. At the centre of the ritual was the communion service in which the Last Supper of Christ was re-enacted. The doctrine of the Roman Catholic Church insisted that **transubstantiation** occurred. This idea was rejected by Protestants who regarded the communion service as purely commemorative of Christ's death. The new wording of the communion service allowed both interpretations to be made: 'Take and eat this in remembrance that Christ died for thee, and feed on him in thy heart by faith with thanksgiving.'

Another area of compromise was the decision on the vestments or ceremonial clothes worn by the clergy. Protestants were generally opposed to the authority of the clergy to intercede between the individual and God and felt that distinctive clothing and church ornaments smacked of popery. Elizabeth, however, was more conservative in this respect and she required that the clergy's authority be respected and insisted that the vestments worn by the clergy should be along traditional lines.

Both the Act of Supremacy and the Act of Uniformity achieved their immediate objectives. A national Protestant Church was set up from which only 300 priests had to be expelled for refusing to take the oath of allegiance. All subjects were expected to attend church and those who did not were fined for **recusancy** or non-attendance. The Settlement was, however, only the beginning and it was uncertain whether a Church designed for the majority would in fact satisfy them all.

KEY TERMS

Transubstantiation – The Roman Catholic doctrine that the priest, by blessing the bread at mass, changes its essence to the body of Christ and the wine to His blood.

Recusant – A Roman Catholic who refuses to attend the services of the Church of England.

Who opposed the Settlement?

It might have been expected that the fiercest opposition would come from the Catholics, but it was the more fervent Protestants who attempted to upset the Settlement. Elizabeth was deeply conscious that the desire to re-establish the old religion had been a crucial factor in the uprisings of 1536 (**The Pilgrimage of Grace**) and 1549 (**The Devon Prayer Book Rebellion**) and she did not want to provoke Catholics into rebellion. Nevertheless, despite the pleas for moderation, some enthusiastic Protestants destroyed statues, ornaments and even vestments and removed altars from churches. Extreme Protestants saw the Settlement as merely a precursor of further reforms whereas Elizabeth felt the need to maintain a balance between competing religious beliefs.

Steering a middle course

To accomplish this balance, Elizabeth wanted to keep some of the Marian bishops, but only one was persuaded to accept office. Most of Elizabeth's bishops were therefore unquestionably Protestant. Indeed, some were so committed to the Protestant cause that they had voluntarily gone into exile rather then live under the Catholic Queen Mary. However, Elizabeth had a free hand with the appointment of a new Archbishop of Canterbury as the see was vacant. She chose Matthew Parker, a moderate who had been a former pupil of Thomas Cranmer and chaplain to her mother Anne Boleyn.

Elizabeth could not persuade Catholics to accept the Settlement but at least she offered tolerance and retained some outward show of their religion in the Church of England services. She was particularly opposed to the marriage of clergy but backed down on this issue after persuasion from Cecil and other Councillors. Most importantly,

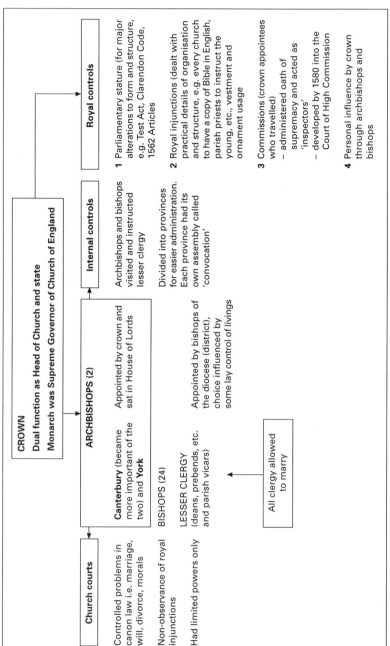

Figure 4 Church structure and discipline

CROWN
Dual function as Head of Church and state
Monarch was Supreme Governor of Church of England

Church courts

Controlled problems in canon law i.e. marriage, will, divorce, morals

Non-observance of royal injunctions

Had limited powers only

Internal controls

Archbishops and bishops visited and instructed lesser clergy

Divided into provinces for easier administration. Each province had its own assembly called 'convocation'

Royal controls

1 Parliamentary stature (for major alterations to form and structure, e.g. Test Act, Clarendon Code, 1562 Articles

2 Royal injunctions (dealt with practical details of organisation and structure, e.g. every church to have a copy of Bible in English, parish priests to instruct the young, etc., vestment and ornament usage

3 Commissions (crown appointees who travelled)
   – administered oath of supremacy and acted as 'inspectors'
   – developed by 1580 into the Court of High Commission

4 Personal influence by crown through archbishops and bishops

ARCHBISHOPS (2)

Canterbury (became more important of the two) and **York**

Appointed by crown and sat in House of Lords

BISHOPS (24)

LESSER CLERGY (deans, prebends, etc. and parish vicars)

Appointed by bishops of the diocese (district), choice influenced by some lay control of livings

All clergy allowed to marry

in the early years of her reign, Catholics were rarely prosecuted for non-attendance at church. If anyone failed to take the Oath of Supremacy the first time, they were not pressed again to take it as refusal could lead to execution.

By insisting that the clergy continue to wear ceremonial costume (vestments), Elizabeth wanted to demonstrate that she did not seek the radical and simple surplice of the Puritans. In 1565 the Queen ordered the clergy to conform to these demands. When 37 priests refused to do so, she insisted that Edmund Grindal, the radical Bishop of London, punish them. Such actions encouraged Catholics to hope that, in time, Elizabeth might be won back to the papal fold. Several books were dedicated to her by exiled Catholics in the hope that flattery would persuade her to support their cause.

In this, however, they were mistaken. As long as her Church was acknowledged, or at least not downright opposed, Elizabeth had no wish to press Catholics further. Elizabeth was Protestant but she hoped that if there were no Catholic martyrs there would be no cause around which to rally. Catholicism, she believed, would gradually fade away and be naturally absorbed into the Church of England. There were also more personal reasons for her retention of some of the outward forms of the old religion. She loved ceremony and believed this was integral to the dignity of her Church. Nor was she someone who could be bullied into submission. By insisting on some of these older practices she was giving a clear signal to her Councillors that she was her own woman. Perhaps instinctively, she knew that many of these practices were what ordinary people cared about, rather than the finer points of theological dispute.

Catholic opposition at home and abroad

Despite Elizabeth's moderate approach, there were English Catholics who were convinced not only that her Church was morally corrupt but that she had no right, as the illegitimate child of Anne Boleyn, to rule. Power politics were thus inextricably linked with matters of religion. The most serious and persistent challenge to Elizabeth came from the claims of Mary Queen of Scots to the English throne. In 1561 Mary had returned to Scotland from France after the death of her husband, the French King Francis II, and so was close enough to England to present a real threat. Scotland, however, had turned to Protestantism and Mary could hardly hope for undivided support from her nobles. What made things dangerous for Elizabeth, though, was that Mary could seek assistance from the powerful Catholic monarchs of France and Spain. But in 1562 civil war broke out in France between Catholics and the Huguenot Protestants, so Mary could not expect help from this quarter.

Elizabeth had more to fear from Philip II of Spain but at this stage he preferred diplomatic overtures, and even proposed marriage at the beginning of her reign. He also hoped that the very vagueness of the Settlement might lead to the re-establishment of papal authority in England, given time.

The Northern Rising

Such hopes were dashed at the close of the 1560s. In 1569 a rebellion was triggered in the north by deteriorating relations between England and Spain. In December 1568, Spanish treasure had been seized (see page 93) and a group of English conservative nobles led by the Duke of Norfolk blamed William Cecil for this diplomatic blunder. Their plan developed into a proposal to name Mary Queen of Scots as Elizabeth's successor and marry her to the Duke of Norfolk, after which she would promptly convert to Protestantism. When things began to get out of hand, Norfolk disassociated himself from the scheme, but not before an uprising had broken out in the north.

Once the vague Protestant ambition had been set aside as an objective of the rebellion, the aim became simply the restoration of the former religion. As in similar cases, however, it masked some naked political ambitions. The rebels were led by the Earls of Northumberland and Westmorland and they asked Spain for assistance.

◢ Source 7

8 Oct. 1569 ... They have sent Northumberland's servant, who spoke to me before on the matter, to say that they will by armed force release the Queen [Mary] and take possession of all the north country, restoring the Catholic religion in this country.

*M. A. S. Hume (ed.), **Calendar of State Papers**, Spanish Volume II; quoted in*
*S. H. P. Holmes, **Elizabethan England** (McDougall, 1977)*

The rising fizzled out but was followed by a far more serious threat the following year. In 1570 the new Pope Pius V was determined to reclaim territory lost to Protestantism. Chief target of his attack was Elizabeth, whom he excommunicated.

◢ Source 8

We do declare that the aforesaid Elizabeth ... to have incurred the sentence of excommunication, and to be cut off from the unity of the body of Christ. And moreover we do declare her to be deprived of her pretended title to the kingdom ... And we do command and charge all and every the noblemen and subjects, people, and others aforesaid that they presume not to obey her or her orders, mandates and laws ...

Papal Bull of Excommunication; quoted in W. Camden, **Annales: The True and Royall History of the famous Empresse Elizabeth, Queen of England France and Ireland, etc. True Faith's Defendresse, of Divine Renowne and Happy Memory** *(1625)*

This was dangerous for it gave English Catholics the legal right to rebel against their monarch. Yet no rebellion took place on any widespread scale. This did not calm fervent Protestants such as Sir Walter Mildmay who warned Parliament in his speech in the House of Commons, 'the dangers be so great, so evident and so imminent' from 'the lewd and malicious enterprises' of the Papists.

Was the Catholic threat real?

Recent historians have suggested that the threats have been overestimated on the basis that:

◢ whilst many Elizabethan courtiers genuinely saw a threat to their beliefs in the machinations of the Pope and foreign princes, they were not above stirring up Catholic 'scare' stories for their own advantage

◢ the majority of the Catholic gentry had no intention of rebelling against Elizabeth but were content to settle for religious toleration as a minority group

◢ those Catholics who advocated conspiracy inflated the numbers of their comrades in order to attract support from France and Spain. The Spanish ambassadors, too, were not above dramatically exaggerating the figures of those waiting for the signal from Spain to throw off the yoke of an alien religion. True conspirators represented only a handful of the population

◢ the missionaries sent to England were few in number, scarcely converted anyone and because they had to rely on members of the aristocracy, could reach only a limited section of the population

◢ curiously, the Catholic Church itself, undergoing its own counter-reformation, was keen to play down the role of saints and elaborate ritual. Yet it was just these features which attracted much of the mass support for the Church amongst ordinary people.

Elizabeth had no intention of conducting a witch hunt against Catholics. Even after the Northern Rising of 1569 she did not insist on using the full rigour of the law against them.

◢ Source 9

Fines were evaded or remained unpaid. ... Elizabeth was not unduly disturbed by these Catholic survivals, so long as they centred round the gentry. In some ways she assisted the process. By her desire, Catholic peers were excused the oath. She did not, on the whole, give them public employment, but she liked to have them at court. In some ways she regarded Catholic peers as supporters of her throne, a balancing factor against the aggressive Protestantism of men like Huntingdon, Bedford and Warwick ... Sometimes she visited the houses of known Catholics.

P. Johnston, *Elizabeth I: A Study in Power and Intellect*
(Weidenfeld and Nicolson, 1974)

Many of her Protestant courtiers did not share her more tolerant attitude to Catholics. In 1582, Leicester wrote, 'Nothing in the world grieveth me more than to see her Majesty believes that this increase of Papists in her realm can be no danger to her.' Why were they so convinced that the Catholics were such a threat? There were three possible reasons:

◢ The existence of plots against Elizabeth – even though they involved only a handful of fanatics, it needed only one successful plot, no matter how crack-brained, to bring about the downfall of the regime. This would mean the probable accession of Mary Queen of Scots, leading to the re-establishment of the Catholic religion.

⊿ Outbreaks of Protestant persecution in France, Spain and the Netherlands – these intensified the desire for revenge and the feeling of isolation of Protestants in England. The massacre of thousands of Huguenots in France on St Bartholomew's Day in 1572 enraged their English co-religionists. Even more threatening, the Pope appeared to give the butchery his blessing. Spanish persecution in the Netherlands was still closer to home and the assassination of William of Orange in 1584 by a Catholic seemed to validate the Pope's threat to heretic rulers.

⊿ Catholic missionary incursions into England – in 1568, William Allen, an English exile in France, founded a seminary in Douai to train Englishmen as priests in order to revitalise Catholicism in their homeland. About 279 priests returned to England over the next six years. The most feared, however, were the Jesuit priests because of their dedication and scholarship. Mildmay expressed his loathing for them, 'creeping into the houses and familiarities of men of behaviour and reputation, not only to corrupt with their false doctrine, but also to stir up sedition to the peril of her Majesty'. Despite the fact that priests had been given strict orders not to interfere in matters of politics, it was impossible to separate out attempts to revive the Catholic faith and to challenge Elizabeth's claim to be the Supreme Governor of the Church of England.

Anti-Catholic laws

It was impossible for Elizabeth to resist these renewed pressures and the treason laws were tightened to deal with the (real or apparent) Catholic threat. After 1571 it was treasonable to bring papal bulls into the country. Anyone who left the country for more than six months was liable to have their land confiscated – a measure aimed at those who trained as priests at Allen's seminary in Douai. From 1575 onwards, the Privy Council launched a campaign against leading Catholic laymen, imprisoning the staunchest adherents, targeting those in Lancashire, Yorkshire and East Anglia where the Catholic faith was strongest. Fines were massively increased by an act of 1581 – for saying mass 200 marks (£133) and imprisonment for one year from a fine of 10 marks previously. Those attending Catholic mass could be fined 100 marks and sentenced to one year's imprisonment.

Non-attendance at church was punishable by a fine of £20 a month from a previous one shilling. Such measures were aimed at warning the gentry not to lead their co-religionists into dissent. More deadly, it became a treasonable offence for anyone to renounce the monarch or to convert someone to Catholicism – in short, priests were traitors and the punishment for treason was a gruesome and terrible death.

Despite the harshness of the laws, English Protestant leaders remained uneasy. Spanish invasion fleets were launched against England in 1588, 1596 and 1597 but the most enduring focus of discontent was the imprisoned Mary Queen of Scots. In 1585, Elizabeth's Councillors were convinced of a real and present danger and in response formed the Bond of Association, whose signatories vowed to pursue to the death anyone who threatened the life of the Queen.

The discovery of the Babington Plot in 1586 provided the opportunity for dealing finally with the problem of Mary. As with previous conspiracies the plan was to murder Elizabeth and replace her with Mary. Mary received information of the plot in letters secretly sent to her by Sir Anthony Babington and agreed to the proposals. Sir Francis Walsingham, Elizabeth's Principal Secretary, discovered the plot early on and allowed Mary to implicate herself before exposing the conspirators. Babington and his comrades were executed but, when it came to Mary, Elizabeth, fearful of the implications of executing a monarch ordained by God, hesitated for almost five months.

Elizabeth finally agreed to Mary's execution in February 1587. Spain had been planning an invasion of England since 1585 and Mary's death provided Philip with the final impetus to attack. An invasion fleet was assembled which attempted to link up with a land army from the Netherlands. It was anticipated that once Spanish soldiers landed a Catholic rebellion would be ignited. The plan failed and English Catholics remained quiescent, having little intention of aiding a foreign invasion force. The threats from Spain remained but Elizabeth now determined upon a policy of limited aid to other troubled areas in support of Protestants fighting against the Catholic League. Eventually she committed 20,000 troops to assist the Protestant French King Henry of Navarre and sent 8,000 soldiers to the Netherlands. The policy proved a success. By 1595 Henry was installed securely as the

King of France and from 1588 onwards the Dutch rebels made consistent progress against the Spanish envoy the Duke of Parma.

Profile SIR FRANCIS WALSINGHAM (1530–90)

Sir Francis Walsingham served Elizabeth for over 20 years as her Principal Secretary. It was probably his connection with the Boleyn family, remote as it was, that brought him to Elizabeth's attention. He was never a favourite of the Queen, being frail and sickly, and his pre-eminence was due to his statecraft. Unlike the Cecils, who tended to be pragmatic and opportunist, Walsingham was a politician of strong convictions.

Like Sir William Cecil, Walsingham was of the new gentry. His family had been members of the shoemakers guild in the early fifteenth century, but by the sixteenth century they had established themselves amongst the country gentry. He fled England when Mary became Queen and studied law at Padua in Italy before joining other Protestant refugees in Germany and Switzerland.

On Elizabeth's accession he served as ambassador to France at a critical time, when the Anglo-Spanish alliance was being supplanted by a rapprochement with France. The St Bartholomew's Day massacre of 1572, however, seriously weakened the new understanding between France and England. In December 1573 he was appointed Elizabeth's Principal Secretary, in which post he remained for 17 years, virtually until the day of his death. Walsingham was, in effect, the managing director of Elizabeth's government, whilst Cecil managed the finances and the Chancellor administered justice. It is a measure of the trust and confidence that Elizabeth had in him that he was never once criticised for his actions. He expressed his hopes as: 'I wish God's glory and next the Queen's safety.' God's glory he interpreted as being the furtherance of the Protestant cause, the defeat of the arch-enemy Spain and the destruction of Mary Queen of Scots. To this end, he established a vast intelligence network of spies who kept him well informed.

What was the Puritan challenge?

The Puritan challenge was of a different order. The Puritans presented no opposition to the claim of Elizabeth to the throne and they were not in league with a foreign power. Many were influenced by the beliefs of Calvin and Zwingli, Protestant reformers in Switzerland. Many had gone into exile during the reign of Mary Tudor, fearing for their lives, but while in exile they had been able to gain first-hand experience of the reforms of these two leading Protestants. When they returned to England during the reign of Elizabeth they exercised considerable influence within the Church of England. The name 'Puritan' probably originated as something of an insult, directed at those who thought they were more deeply religious than their neighbours and obsessed with 'purifying' the English Church. They disliked ceremony and ritual and many saw little need for a priest to act as an intermediary between them and God.

The term 'Puritan' was used as one of abuse but it could be interpreted as an insult in several different ways:

- in a religious sense the term 'Puritan' meant a Protestant radical who demanded reforms in the Church, 'a hotter sort of Protestant' in contemporary terms
- in a moral sense it indicated someone who was narrow-minded, intensely critical of other people's behaviour
- in a social sense it was sometimes used to indicate that a person was no gentleman, 'a mean person'. As followers of Calvin, Puritans saw themselves forever battling against a corrupt and ungodly world. They criticised the Elizabethan Religious Settlement as 'but halfly reformed' and regarded the establishment of the Anglican Church as a 'cloaked papistry or a mingle-mangle' (*Device for the Alteration of Religion, 1558*).

In 1566 a combination of radical councillors, MPs and bishops produced some suggestions for further reform within the Church of England:

◢ Source 10

- *That all Sundays in the year and the principal feasts of Christ be kept holy days; and all other holy days be abrogated* [abolished]
- *That in all parish churches the minister in common prayer turn his face towards the people; and there distinctly read the divine service appointed where all the people assembled may hear and be edified*
- *That in ministering the sacrament* [anointing using Christ's name] *of baptism, the*

ceremony of making the cross in the child's forehead may be omitted as tending to superstitious

* *That the use of organs be removed*

*Some Puritan suggestions for reform of the Church of England in the Articles of Convocation, 1563; quoted in S. H. P. Holmes, **Elizabethan England** (McDougall, 1977)*

Reasons for Puritan opposition to the Settlement

From a list of their requests it can be seen that the Puritans saw the Settlement as a flawed compromise which needed amendment. Furthermore, they continually attacked what they considered to be poor-quality clergy. Their criticism fell into two parts:

◢ Administration – Elizabeth desired an orderly Church with a clear chain of command. Puritan critics saw in the bishops and other office holders a perpetuation of the Catholic Church hierarchy. They wanted inspirational leaders who sought their authority in the Bible, not in the state. At the radical end of the Puritan movement were sects such as the Separatists or Brownists (after their founder, Robert Brown), who believed in the complete separation of Church and state, with each congregation determining its own practices. In this case they could never belong to a Church that was controlled by the state although they did exert pressure for reform within it.

◢ Liturgy (the form worship took) – the Puritans wanted to remove any artefact or ritual that reminded them of Roman Catholic practice. They objected to statues, ceremonial dress (vestments), making the sign of the cross and celebration of saints' days, which they dismissed as 'insinuate foolery, and new remembrance of heathen idolatry'. In their view, too few priests were preachers dedicated enough to be 'diligent barkers against the papish wolf'.

Elizabeth's attitude to Puritans

Elizabeth recognised that Puritan emphasis on individual salvation and self-governing churches was a direct challenge to her status as Supreme Governor of the Church of England. In her opinion, the Puritans were 'divided amongst themselves with a variety of dangerous opinion', which would split her Church from stem to stern.

This did not deter her, however, from placing dedicated Puritans at the heart of government, for example Leicester, his brother the Earl of Warwick, the earls of Huntingdon and Bedford, and Francis Walsingham. Such powerful figures blunted attacks against the movement as well as protected individuals.

But clashes were bound to come.

◢ The Vestment or Vestiarian Controversy of the 1560s. To stern Protestants ceremonial dress was 'a filthy popish rag'. The Puritanical Dean of Wells, Dr Peter Turner, was so incensed at the square caps the clergy were ordered to wear that he trained his pet dog to leap up and snatch the caps off the heads of passing clergy. In the first few years of the Settlement vestments did not emerge as a contentious issue as the Settlement was laxly enforced. By the beginning of 1565, Elizabeth had become increasingly disturbed at the lack of uniformity amongst the clergy and gave instructions to Archbishop Parker and the bishops that they must set their house in order. In March, Parker set out a detailed dress code which all ministers were expected to follow.

Two leading opponents of vestments, Laurence Humphrey, Regius Professor of Divinity at Oxford, and Thomas Sampson, the Dean of Christchurch, led the resistance, vowing never to wear the cap and surplice. Sampson was deprived of his post and Humphrey banned from lecturing. In March 1566, Matthew Parker issued the 'Advertisements' which explained the reasons for conformity in dress when 37 London ministers were suspended for refusing to wear the prescribed dress. After three months all but three had conformed.

◢ Presbyterianism. The Cambridge Professor of Divinity, Thomas Cartwright, gave a series of lectures in which he maintained that there was no basis in scripture for the government of the Church by bishops. Cartwright advocated that instead its administration should be by ministers, deacons and lay elders or presbytery. At the end of the year he was dismissed from his post and he fled to Germany to escape probable arrest.

◢ Reform of the Book of Common Prayer. In 1571, Walter Strickland proposed a bill to recommend improvements to the Book of Common Prayer. Elizabeth made her attitude to this proposal crystal clear in 1572 when she declared at the reassembly of Parliament, 'henceforth no bills concerning religion should be received into this House unless the same should be first liked by the clergy'. She knew of course that the bishops would knock this proposal on the head as they had done in the House of Lords. Strickland was imprisoned as a further warning to like-minded supporters. In frustration, two Puritan militants, John Field and Thomas Wilcox, produced a virulent attack on bishops in a pamphlet called *Admonition to Parliament*. Field and Wilcox were jailed for a year but this did not prevent the tract becoming a popular success.

◢ Prophesying. In May 1575 Archbishop Parker died and was replaced by the Archbishop of York, Edmund Grindal. The appointment was something of a surprise as he was one of the more radical members of the episcopate. It was hoped that he would unite the Church. Instead he clashed with Elizabeth almost immediately. As the Church was short of trained ministers, meetings called 'prophesyings' were held to discuss the scriptures. It was hoped this method would improve the quality of ministers. These meetings were not radical assemblies but Elizabeth viewed them all with suspicion, and whilst it was true that Puritans usually took a lead in them, she was convinced that they were the basis for a radical Puritan network. She summoned Grindal in 1576 and told him that the prophesyings must be banned. Grindal refused to obey her orders and was suspended from his post, although he technically remained in office until his death in 1583.

◢ Presbyterianism. Elizabeth had to wait until the death of Grindal before renewing the attack on Puritans. Presbyteries were assemblies of ministers and church elders who governed each congregation and were a small, but articulate and vocal group. In Scotland, they had taken root as a form of devolved Church government. In 1583, Elizabeth appointed John Whitgift as Archbishop of Canterbury and gave him strict instructions that conformity to the Settlement was required of all clergy. This nearly led to the dismissal of 300 ministers until the intervention of

Leicester, who argued that the Church could not afford to lose such stalwarts at a time when they were facing vehement Catholic opposition.

By 1585 Elizabeth had held her ground and Puritans could expect no concessions, but whilst the Puritans were more quiescent in the face of a perceived Catholic threat they had by no means abandoned their aims.

Was the Religious Settlement a triumph?

Elizabeth's Religious Settlement of 1559 lasted without fundamental change until the end of her reign, spanning almost two generations. Catholics had been clearly opposed to the Settlement from the outset but because Elizabeth did not enforce conformity amongst them, conspiracies against her regime were few and supported by only a handful of disaffected gentry. This is despite the venomous attacks upon her from the pen of critics such as William Allen, who described her as 'an incestuous bastard, begotten and born in sinne of an infamous courtesan', as well as the physical assaults on her realm by Spain. This did not mean that the fear of a Catholic uprising passed away. 88, mostly lay Catholics were executed for opposition to the government between 1590 and 1603. But as 1588 receded, the threat of a Catholic insurrection grew fainter.

Puritans, on the other hand, thought of the Settlement as merely a prelude to greater reform. Elizabeth's long reign enabled the continuity of the Protestant religion and the Settlement to be sustained. More complex matters of doctrine were resolved in the latter part of Elizabeth's reign but the basic form and shape of the established Church was not altered. Puritans, however, did not dilute their demands. In 1586 a Star Chamber decree was issued, ordering the destruction of unauthorised printing presses, a measure directed at curtailing Puritan pamphleteering. No book was to be published without the permission of the Archbishop of Canterbury or the Bishop of London. Puritans fought back in the Parliament of 1586–7 with a bill introduced by Anthony Cope, designed to replace the Book of Common Prayer and totally reconstruct the Church of England along

Presbyterian lines. Cope and his supporters were immediately imprisoned. Whilst many MPs were sympathetic to moderate Puritan views they had no intention of implementing them if it meant sacrificing the national Church – a Church of England – a symbol of their nationhood.

Elizabeth's reign witnessed a remarkable shift in popular religion from Catholicism to moderate Protestantism to which the vast majority of the population subscribed. Why was this so?

◢ Interference from outside England was resented – in this sense the Pope was regarded as an intruder by many Englishmen, particularly so once regionalism began to be superseded by a pride in English achievement.

◢ The Settlement trod a moderate path, retaining elements of the ceremonies and rituals in order to encourage widespread support.

◢ The gradual improvement in the quality and sincerity of many Protestant preachers and vicars established the credibility of the Protestant religion.

◢ The increasing number of graduates coming into the ministry meant that the Puritans no longer had a monopoly on learning.

Evaluation and interpretation of sources

As a general strategy, when evaluating a source always start from the simple and move to the complex; always start from the outside and move inwards by:

- underlining and explaining difficult words
- decoding key words
- determining who has written it, when, to whom and for what reason
- looking at the tone of the text – why has the author used particular words and phrases?
- analysing whether it differs from other sources.

Taking these points into consideration, read the sources as directed and answer the questions below.

1 Study Source 1.
   a How does Count von Helffstein compliment Elizabeth on her handling of religious divisions?
   b Is his view borne out by subsequent events during Elizabeth's reign?
   c How might you modify, if you thought it necessary, the judgement of Count von Helffstein?
   d Does this source indicate that he supported her Settlement? What else would you need to know to make a better-informed decision?

2 Read Sources 2, 3 and 4. In what way do these extracts demonstrate:
   a depth of feeling?
   b the extent to which religion pervaded individual lives and the machinery of state?

3 Read Sources 5 and 6.
   a In what way does the N. L. Jones's interpretation differ from that of J. E. Neale?
   b Does the extract from J. Loach's book support or reject N. L. Jones's interpretation?
   c What difficulties are there in coming to a definite conclusion regarding Elizabeth's intentions?

TASKS

4 Read Sources 7, 8 and 9.

  a In what ways do these sources identify fundamental threats to Elizabeth's reign?

  b In what way do the instructions in Source 8 represent a significant threat to Elizabeth's reign?

  c As a consequence of what you have read in Source 8, how might Northumberland argue that he is acting legally?

  d In what way does Source 9 demonstrate Elizabeth's:

    ◢ religious belief?

    ◢ statehood?

    ◢ personal temperament?

  e How did Elizabeth ensure that Northumberland and other conspirators did not achieve widespread support from other Catholic gentry?

5 Read Source 10.

  a What common features of Puritan belief can be found in this source?

  b How might these features bring Puritans into conflict with Elizabeth's Settlement?

Extended writing tasks

To analyse a question, you need to decide:

a which are the operative words, e.g. describe, explain, assess, how, why, to what extent.

b what are the scope and limitations of the question?

Example: **Describe what was meant by the 'Royal Prerogative'. How were attempts to limit the Prerogative defeated by the crown during Elizabeth's reign? How effective were the attempts to limit the Royal Prerogative?**

Operative words	Analysis	Scope and limitations
a Describe	Define Prerogative – with examples (always give examples)	No determining dates so cover all reign

| **b** How were | Description of methods used to defeat opposition – with examples | Prerogative powers only |
| **c** How effective | Present a case: contrast powers lost with those kept – make judgement on effectiveness – examples needed as 'evidence' | Limitations, if any |

Structuring your answers

Make a brief plan of the areas you will cover – a few lines in a few minutes. Don't write out a rough draft! Cross out the plan when you have finished the essay.

◢ The different sections of each essay question are an agenda for the complete essay. So you are writing ONE essay, not two or three mini essays.

◢ You should write a brief introduction and conclusion to the whole essay (covering all the parts).

◢ It helps if you separate each of the sub-sections, e.g. by leaving a line between them.

Example: **What was the nature of the offence known as recusancy? How effective were the recusancy laws in the reign of Elizabeth? To what extent were they used as an instrument of political, rather than religious, control?**

Introduction In Tudor England, the concept of 'one state, one religion' had to be enforced largely for reasons of security. When Elizabeth moved the state religion away from Rome in 1559 there were, naturally, many subjects who had to be coerced to the new religion.

Topic sentence **a** The recusancy laws (more correctly called the penal laws) were introduced to encourage Catholics to pay lip service to the Church of England. Thus it was an offence to … (points developed)

Topic sentence **b** Despite these laws, Catholicism did not die out in England. The extent to which Catholics conformed outwardly only, to the state religion, can be measured by ... (points developed)

Topic sentence **c** The view that the recusancy laws were essentially developed as a political weapon, rather than arising from religious concerns, is demonstrated by the fact that the laws were enforced much more vigorously in times of political crisis. For example ... (points developed)

Conclusion Thus it can be seen that the Catholic subjects of Elizabeth were initially treated leniently and many continued to practise their religion. But circumstances at home and abroad often put Catholics in the position of traitors to their Queen. It was in these times that political action was taken to ensure the security of the state.

Remember to give examples for each general point. EVIDENCE IS REQUIRED!

Using the essay question above:
a What are the operative words?
b What is each section requiring you to do (e.g. define, analyse, etc.)?
c What clues are given to the scope and limitations of each section (e.g. only concerns Catholicism)?

A number of extended writing tasks are listed below. Select one or more and provide a plan based on the examples given above.

1 What were the problems Elizabeth faced in re-establishing Protestantism in 1559 and how were they solved?
2 What were Elizabeth's original intentions concerning the Religious Settlement? How did foreign affairs affect the Settlement?
3 What was the Commons' attitude to royal supremacy in Church government?
4 Who were the Puritans and why were they regarded as a threat to Elizabeth's Religious Settlement?
5 Why was Mary Stuart so important a factor in matters of state and religion? Which plots was she the focus of and what were the aims of the plotters?

TASKS

6 How would the Northern Rising have benefited Catholicism if it had succeeded?

7 What effect did the publication of the Papal Bull of Excommunication of 1570 have on English Catholicism?

8 In 1566, Archbishop Parker published his 'Advertisements'. This gave rise to the Vestiarian Controversy. What was the reason for the argument and how did it create constitutional problems?

9 'Presbyterianism was strongest in 1587. Six years later it had ceased to exist.' What were the origins and aims of the movement and what were the reasons for its sudden decline?

10 'Prophesyings' were popular 'Bible Study' groups. Why did the Queen disapprove and what steps were taken to stop them?

11 'The Religious Settlement of 1559 was a triumph.' To what extent would you agree with this conclusion?

CHAPTER TWO

ELIZABETH AND HER PARLIAMENTS – A MARRIAGE OF CONVENIENCE?

Objectives

⊿ To understand the reasons why Parliament was called
⊿ To show how Parliament was managed
⊿ To examine the relationship between the Houses of Parliament and the Privy Council
⊿ To study opposition to the crown and how this has been interpreted.

You will know that Parliament was much weaker in Tudor times than it is now and that it only operated at the monarch's request. However, do not assume that the crown felt it could dispense with Parliaments when it chose. No one considered government was possible without it. The following chart shows:

⊿ when Elizabeth's Parliaments were called and their duration
⊿ the main issues discussed by Parliament and the decisions reached
⊿ the nature of the opposition (if any) and its outcome.

Parliaments, 1558–68	
25 January – 8 May 1559	To determine the Religious Settlement for the Church of England – Opposition from Roman Catholic bishops in the House of Lords – Two ringleaders imprisoned in the Tower. The Acts of Supremacy and Uniformity passed. Subsidy granted to the crown.
12 January – 10 April 1563	To discuss whether England should aid Scottish rebels against the French regency. Subsidy granted to the crown.
13 September 1566 – 2 January 1567	To discuss whether England should assist the Protestant Huguenot rebels in France. Subsidy granted to the crown.

Summary

Elizabeth's first Parliament was dominated by the need to find a religious settlement. Another urgent consideration was the need, common to all monarchs, to gain Parliamentary subsidies in order to finance government. England was still at war with France and wars always place considerable financial strains on a country. Bearing this in mind, Elizabeth was persuaded to back Protestants abroad only if there was a clear national interest involved.

Parliaments, 1568–85

2 April – 29 May 1571	To discuss the response to the Northern Rising. The Pope's excommunication of Elizabeth. Subsidy granted to the crown.
8 May – 13 June 1572	To discuss the fate of Mary Queen of Scots.
8 February – 15 March 1576	Subsidy granted to the crown.
16 January – 18 March 1581	To pass harsher anti-Catholic laws. To discuss the secret arrival of Jesuit priests in England. The reaction to Philip II of Spain's accession to the throne of Portugal. Subsidy granted to the crown.
23 November 1584 – 29 March 1585	To discuss security measures after plots had been discovered against Elizabeth, following the recent assassination of the Protestant William of Orange. Subsidy granted to the crown.

Summary

This was generally a period of considerable co-operation, with one or two exceptional outbursts in which Elizabeth's views were challenged. One line of protest came from the Queen's Councillors themselves who were looking to use Parliament as a means of putting pressure on Elizabeth, much to her irritation. They raised the succession question and hoped to persuade Elizabeth to take decisive action against Mary Queen of Scots. Another challenge to the Queen came from one or two individuals who questioned the basis of the relationship between monarch and Parliament. Peter Wentworth was in the forefront of these attacks upon the monarch's power, although he received negligible support from the other MPs.

Parliaments, 1585–1603

29 October 1586 – 23 March 1587	To discuss the need for Mary Queen of Scots' execution – resisted by Elizabeth. Attempt by Anthony Cope and leading Protestants to repeal all existing legislation in their favour. Wentworth speaks in favour of Cope and is sent to the Tower. Subsidy granted to the crown.
4 February – 29 March 1589	Double subsidy granted to the crown to wage war against Spain. House of Commons challenges Elizabeth over purveyance (the right of the crown to buy provisions at fixed low prices) – Elizabeth exercises Royal Prerogative and quashes the bill.
19 February – 10 April 1593	Three subsidies granted to the crown. Some Puritan agitation but suppressed. Wentworth raises issue of succession – expelled by the House of Commons and imprisoned in the Tower where he dies a few years later.
24 October 1597 – 9 February 1598	Triple subsidy granted to the crown. Legislation passed for the relief of the poor and the punishment of vagabonds. Attacks on crown's right to grant monopolies. Subsidy granted to the crown.
27 October – 19 December 1601	Further attacks on the rights of the crown to grant monopolies – Elizabeth pacifies Parliament. Quadruple subsidies granted to crown despite some opposition.

Summary

Elizabeth was reluctant to call Parliaments except in cases of financial necessity. It should be added that many MPs shared her view, for travel to London was uncomfortable and hazardous. Tensions became more pronounced in the final years of her reign. The Parliament of 1586–7 was extremely lively. On the one hand members were baying for Mary Queen of Scots' blood and on the other, Puritans, led by Sir Anthony Cope, were demanding the repeal of the Act of Uniformity and the establishment of a more extreme Protestant settlement. Elizabeth still wavered over Mary's fate. She was strongly opposed to Cope for she feared the delicate balance achieved in the Settlement would be upset. Her particular anger was reserved for Wentworth who challenged her Prerogative in Parliament. He was sent to the Tower for his pains.

As the war with Spain progressed, Elizabeth required greater subsidies so that her requests were first doubled and then trebled. Elizabeth was challenged over purveyance – the right to purchase commodities for the court and to commandeer transport at lower than the prevailing market prices – but she refused to give Royal Assent to the bill. Although feelings ran high over this issue, the Queen managed to defuse the situation by organising working parties to discuss the matter.

In the Parliament of 1593, the Lords offered a triple subsidy, increasing the double subsidy granted by the Commons. This appeared to question the Commons' tax-raising powers. Elizabeth managed to soothe their ruffled feathers.

Renewed Puritan agitation received little support and a bill was passed against the radical Puritans, the Separatists, who were demanding the disestablishment of the Church of England. Wentworth was active again, this time insisting on a decision over the succession. Unsuccessful again, he was put in prison, where he died a few years later. Triple subsidies were granted by the 1597–8 Parliament, despite economic recession, to fund the continuing war with Spain and the expedition to put down the rebellion in Ireland. Poverty and hardship also prompted the government to legislate against vagabonds and to frame the Poor Law regulations. Monopolies came under attack from the Commons, posing the most serious threat to the Queen. Yet the issue was taken up again in the final Parliament of Elizabeth's reign, but she handled the trouble deftly, promising an enquiry into the practice. Parliament also granted the Queen a quadruple subsidy.

Overview
Parliament, unlike the Privy Council, met only intermittently. Elizabeth summoned only 10 Parliaments which sat for 13 sessions and in total lasted only 126 weeks out of a 44-year reign. Elizabeth prided herself on the infrequent calling of Parliament, as she was to inform the Lords and Commons through the Lord Keeper in 1593: 'Her majesty hath evermore been loth to call for the assembly of her people in Parliament, and hath done the same but rarely and only upon most just, weighty and great occasions.' Considering the hardships and perils of travel at the time, this was a view shared by many MPs.

Whilst Parliament debated bills and enacted laws on issues of major concern to the country, it was also a forum where mundane matters were settled. Parliament was equally concerned with minor issues, as the following selection of bills from the 1581 Parliament demonstrates:

- two bills for the paving of streets
- a bill to extend a statute concerning hats and caps
- a bill from the Lords that speakers of slanderous words against the Queen's majesty should be set upon the pillory, lose their ears and suffer imprisonment at the Queen's pleasure.

Reasons for calling Parliament

The most overwhelming reason for the crown to call Parliament was the need to raise money to supplement the monarch's normal revenue. Sir John Fortescue had established the distinction between **ordinary** and **extra-ordinary expenditure** in his treatise '**The Governance**' in the last quarter of the fifteenth century. Ordinary expenditure included royal revenues from crown lands, profits of justice, customs duties and feudal dues. The crown's ordinary expenses were required to meet the costs of the royal household, salaries of officials, the maintenance of law courts and the royal houses and castles.

The crown was always chronically short of money, particularly when waging war. It was accepted that taxation to meet these extra-ordinary demands required Parliamentary consent. Subsidies to meet these costs were the subject of every Parliament.

Although the monarch had the power to issue proclamations which had the force of law, by Elizabeth's reign it was acknowledged that Parliamentary statute had greater authority. This increased status had emerged during the fifteenth century but particularly during the 1529–36 Reformation Parliament of Henry VIII. It gave the stamp of approval to crown policy by enlisting the support of all the governing classes. Questions of religion, frequently entangled with plots against the monarch and support for foreign Protestants, were also frequent topics for debate and legislation. Opposition to royal policies was diverse, sporadic and easily dealt with, although the later opposition to the crown's right to grant monopolies began to take on a serious and concerted character towards the end of Elizabeth's reign.

How did Elizabeth maintain her control of Parliament?

Parliament had the power to pass statutes or laws, to grant subsidies for extra-ordinary expenditure and to impeach or bring to trial powerful advisers to the crown (although this latter right was never exercised during the Tudor period). But it had little control over the levers of power. Monarchs could summon, prorogue (adjourn) and dissolve Parliaments as they wished. Furthermore, monarchs had to assent to all laws before they could become statute and could suspend or dispense with them as they chose. In the 1559 Parliament, for example, Elizabeth instructed MPs in the principal reason for their summons:

◢ Source 1

Now the matters and causes whereupon you are to consult, are chiefly and principally three points. Of those the first is of well making of a uniform order of religion, to the honour and glory of God, the establishing of the Church, and tranquillity of the realm.

Simonds D'Ewes (ed.), **The Journals of all the Parliaments during the reign of Queen Elizabeth**, revised and published by Paul Bowes (1682)

Laws passed were invariably initiated by the crown through members of the Privy Council (page 21). Privy Councillors sat in both the House of Commons and the Lords, controlling the business and initiating legislation. The great majority of minor bills, however, were promoted by private members. The Speaker played a crucial role in managing the business of the Commons and the crown always ensured that his influence was exercised on its behalf.

◢ Source 2

Mr Treasurer of the Queen's house, standing up uncovered did first put the House in remembrance of ... her Majesty's pleasure that they should choose a Speaker ... he thought it his duty to take that occasion to commend to their choice, Sir Thomas Gargrave ... he said he did not intend to debar any other there present, from uttering their free opinions, and nominating any other whom they thought to be more fitting ... They did with one voice and consent, allow and approve of Mr Treasurer's nomination and elected the said Sir Thomas Gargrave ...

Simonds D'Ewes (ed.), **The Journals of all the Parliaments during the reign of Queen Elizabeth**, revised and published by Paul Bowes (1682)

The Privy Council was therefore an important bridge between the crown and Parliament. The Privy Council met regularly and had the advantage of ensuring continuity of policy. Disagreements were usually confined within the Privy Council rather than being aired in Parliament. When issues were raised in Parliament they were quite often engineered by Elizabeth's Councillors as a means of pressing her into making decisions which she preferred to defer, for example the question of succession or the fate of Mary Queen of Scots. Elizabeth was adept at keeping such disputes under control and never giving the impression that she favoured one view over another, often to the bitter frustration of her Councillors.

◢ Source 3

Leicester, Hatton and Walsingham have endeavoured to persuade the Queen that it is desirable for her openly to take the states [Netherlands] under protection ... but they have been opposed by Cecil and Sussex when the matter was discussed in the Council, and the question therefore remained undecided.

> *M. A. S. Hume (ed.),* **Calendar of State Papers***, Spanish Volume III Elizabeth; quoted in*
> *S. H. P. Holmes,* **Elizabethan England** *(McDougall, 1977)*

Elizabeth, for the most part, was skilled at handling these conflicts of interest, playing off one against the other and refusing to allow any single Councillor to dominate the Council as a whole:

◢ Source 4

Her ministers and instruments of State ... were many, and those memorable; but they were only favourites, and not minions; such as acted more by princely rules and judgements, than by their own wills and appetites ...

The principal note of her reign will be, that she ruled much by faction and parties, which she herself both made, upheld, and weakened, as her own great judgement advised ...

> *Sir Robert Naunton,* **Fragmentia Regalia** *(London, 1641); quoted in*
> *S. H. P. Holmes,* **Elizabethan England** *(McDougall, 1977)*

In the latter part of Elizabeth's reign her tight grip on the Privy Council proceedings slackened and the rivalry between ROBERT DEVEREUX, EARL OF ESSEX, and ROBERT CECIL, EARL OF SALISBURY came to a head in a revolt by Essex. Frequently, Elizabeth took credit when things went well and attributed the blunders to others when things went badly.

Profile ROBERT DEVEREUX, EARL OF ESSEX (1569–1601)

In the last years of his life Leicester introduced his young step-son, Robert Devereux, Earl of Essex, to the court. By the age of 18 Essex had established himself as the Queen's favourite. Their friendship was peppered with quarrels and reconciliations. In 1589, against Elizabeth's wishes, he joined the expedition to Portugal. On his return, he was forgiven. This set a pattern for their future relationship. At 23 he risked the Queen's anger by marrying Frances Sidney, the daughter of Sir Francis Walsingham, without Elizabeth's consent. Predictably she flew into a rage, but within a fortnight Essex was forgiven.

As the Portuguese expedition demonstrated, Essex was ambitious to gain military glory and political influence. In 1595 he was made a Privy Councillor and soon earned a reputation as master of detail in foreign policy. In 1596 Essex was given the opportunity to gain military glory by being placed in joint command of a raid on Cadiz. The expedition was successful and he returned as a popular hero. The failure of a further expedition to the Azores seemed to do little to tarnish his image in the sight of Elizabeth.

Essex's downfall was enmeshed in Elizabeth's attempt to dominate Ireland militarily. Put in charge of an expeditionary force to Ireland in 1599, he dawdled and allowed his army to be whittled away by disease and desertion. Abandoning his army, he rushed to London to plead his case. Elizabeth allowed him to return to his home but he was forbidden to appear at court again. Bereft of his offices and in financial straits he encouraged rebellion. After the attempt had petered into farce, Essex was tried, condemned and executed in 1601.

Profile ROBERT CECIL, EARL OF SALISBURY (1563–1612)

Robert Cecil was the son of William Cecil. He entered government service in 1584 when he was sent as part of Lord Derby's delegation to negotiate peace with Spain. In 1591 he received a knighthood and was appointed to the Privy Council, but not until 1596, at the time of the Cadiz expedition, was he made Secretary of State. In 1598, Philip II, wearied by his long succession of humiliating reverses, attempted an alliance with Henry IV of France. Cecil was quick to react to the danger this presented to England and organised an embassy to prevent the alliance being formed.

When Essex returned to England after abandoning his army in Ireland, Cecil was one of the 18 Commissioners who sat on 5 June 1600 to try him for this offence. It was through Cecil's discreet intercession that Essex was allowed his liberty, though forbidden to attend court. Essex later accused Cecil of having organised the campaign against him.

In the last years of Elizabeth's reign, Cecil did much to ensure the safe succession of James VI of Scotland as James I of England. This was done in much secrecy and as a reward he continued in office under the new King.

◢ **Source 5**

Her wisest and best Councillors were oft sore troubled to know her will in matters of state; so covertly did she pass her judgement, as seemed to leave all to their discreet management; and, when the business did turn to better advantage, she did most cunningly commit the good issue to her own honour and understanding; but, when aught fell out contrary to her will and interest, the Council were in great strait to defend their own acting and not blemish the Queen's judgement.

*J. Harington, **Nugae Antiquae** Volume I (London, 1804)*

Opposition within Parliament

Only exceptionally was the view of the 'political nation' (a nation-state united under and by the monarch) challenged when some MPs laid claim to particular rights and privileges. Elizabeth was at pains to stress that MPs should speak their opinion but only within the constraints of the issues laid before the Houses and certainly not to question the basic tenets of government.

◢ Source 6

For liberty of speech her Majesty commandeth me to tell you that to say yea or no to bills, God forbiddeth that any man should be restrained or afraid to answer according to his best liking, with some short declaration of his reason therein, and therein to have a free voice, which is the very true liberty of the House; not, as some suppose, to speak there of all causes as him listeth, and to frame a form of religion or a state of government as to their idle brains shall seem meetest. She sayeth no king fit for his state will suffer such absurdities ...

> J. E. Neale, 'The Lord Keeper's speech to Parliament, 1592–3'
> in **The English Historical Review**, xxxi (1916)

◢ Source 7

I saw [in the last Parliament] the liberty of free speech, which is only salve to heal all the sores of this commonwealth, so much and so many ways infringed ... that my mind hath not been a little aggrieved even of the very conscience and love to my prince and state ...

Amongst other, Mr Speaker, two things do very great hurt in this place of which I mean to speak. One is the rumour that runs about the House and it is 'take heed what you do, the Queen's majesty likes not such a matter; whoever prefers it, she will be much offended with him' ... The other is sometimes a message is brought into the House commanding or inhibiting, or injurious to the freedom of speech and consultation. I would to God, Mr Speaker, that these two were buried in Hell ... [God] did put it into the Queen Majesty's heart to refuse good and wholesome laws for her own preservation, which caused many faithful hearts for grief to burst out with sorrowful tears and moved all papists ... in their sleeves to laugh all the Parliament house to scorn ... none is without fault, no, not our noble Queen. Since then her Majesty has committed great faults, dangerous to herself and the state ... these they are. It is a dangerous thing in a prince unkindly to treat and abuse his or her nobility and people as her Majesty did in the last Parliament ...

> Extracts from Peter Wentworth's speech in the House of Commons, 8 February 1576;
> quoted in I. Dawson, **The Tudor Century 1485–1603** (Nelson, 1993)

Even Peter Wentworth's challenge, which accused Elizabeth of muzzling Parliament, was regarded by the majority of MPs as representative of only a restive few. Speaker Sir William Puckering closed the session by declaring:

◢ Source 8

... some very few members have fallen and offended, rather by infirmity of judgement and through preposterous zeal, than of any disobedience to our better proceedings; yet, generally, the whole number hath from time to time no less readily assembled than quietly conferred and painfully travailled ...

J. E. Neale, 'The Lord Keeper's speech to Parliament, 1592–3'
in **The English Historical Review**, xxxi (1916)

Wentworth's questioning of the basic assumptions upon which government rested clearly angered the Queen, but it must be remembered that it also shocked the majority of members who promptly expelled him from the Commons for his temerity. He was imprisoned on this occasion. When he again accused the Queen of muzzling the Commons over Cope's bill in 1587 he was sent to the Tower (page 57).

The Queen could also resort to clear legal precedents such as her power to call, adjourn or dissolve Parliament, to veto bills and to dispense with unwelcome laws, as well as the right to formulate and initiate policy on such matters as marriage, succession, religion and foreign policy. Elizabeth preferred, however, to manipulate opinion, employing flattery, persuasion and shrewd political tactics to get her own way. In this way she avoided stirring up further antagonisms. As a last resort, and one she used sparingly, she could and did curtail freedom of speech in Parliament by imprisonment, if, in her opinion, members went too far. Towards the end of her reign her disputes with Parliament began to increase, much to her distress. But it says much about her political craft that through a combination of charm and stubbornness she prevented disputes from escalating into open conflict.

Interpretations of Elizabeth's Parliaments

J. E. Neale and the Parliamentary opposition debate

Some historians have argued that Parliament became heavily politicised during this period. Foremost among those historians who hold this view was J. E. Neale (*Queen Elizabeth I*, Jonathan Cape, 1934) who believed that Tudor Parliaments had evolved from ill-defined beginnings in the Middle Ages to maturity under Elizabeth, leading ultimately to civil conflict during the seventeenth century and to the execution of Charles I.

Neale's case rested upon the following interpretations of events under Elizabeth:

- a rise in the power of the House of Commons which challenged the Privy Council and the monarch
- assistance from the House of Lords for the monarchy against the rising tide of the House of Commons
- growth of a coherent Puritan opposition within Parliament who used the institution to promote their religious views
- subsidy grants which were used as levers to obtain concessions from the monarch.

Criticisms of J. E. Neale's interpretation

Neale was not entirely wrong in his assertions. The Commons did witness a rise in the number of representatives of the gentry (302 in 1512, 402 in 1559, 438 in 1571, 462 in 1586) whereas the Lords remained fairly constant at between 75 and 88 members. But this did not mean that the Commons identified itself as a distinct group whose interests were markedly different from those of the peers and the monarch. On the contrary; the Commons was inextricably bound to the system of court and shire, which the nobility dominated.

Many of the errors that Neale fell into were determined when he attributed the causes of later events to the period of the Civil War 1641–9.

But Neale's arguments were seriously flawed. From an examination of the Parliamentary records of both Houses, taken in conjunction with the discussions of the Privy Council, a different picture emerges. The Queen, Lords and Commons were partners in the legislative process. As we have seen, Parliaments were regarded as harmonious elements in the political nation in which conflicts were the exception rather than the norm.

When arguments did occur, their source was often the Privy Council or the court, and Parliament was used to exerting pressure on the Queen. This was the case in the debates on the succession in 1563 and 1566; on religion in 1571; on the fate of Mary Queen of Scots in 1572 and 1586–7; and on the Bond of Association in 1584–5. In 1571 a group of prominent MPs wished six bills to enforce the Thirty-Nine Articles, defining the creed of the Anglican Church, more rigorously. The Church liturgy was enshrined in the Book of Common Prayer and represented a compromise whereby the bishops (episcopacy), vestments and Church discipline were retained. In doctrinal terms, it followed Calvinist teaching by abolishing the mass and discarding transubstantiation. The Queen intervened and allowed two lesser bills to be passed. Elizabeth acted similarly in 1572 when two bills concerning the fate of Mary Queen of Scots foundered. In 1586 she stopped Burghley in his attempt to force a declaration of the succession question. In 1571 and 1593 she stated categorically that Parliament had no right to discuss matters of state unless introduced by herself.

Nor was the House of Lords on the retreat from the power of the House of Commons during Elizabeth's reign. The records show it to have taken an active part in Parliamentary debates, its attendance record at sessions outstripping that of the Commons. The Lords' social pre-eminence ensured that they were closer to court circles and therefore could dominate their clients in the Commons. Furthermore, individual peers were capable of challenging the wishes of the monarch, as seen in the bishops' opposition to the Religious Settlement of 1559.

The Commons was powerless to act on its own for it could do nothing without the agreement of the House of Lords. In the 1589 Parliament the Commons passed two bills which touched on the Royal Prerogative. The Lords refused to accept the bills and there the matter ended.

◢ Source 9

Many of their [aristocratic] clients were elected to the Commons by their good offices and they were likely to be of similar political opinion and religious persuasion to their patrons … In the campaigns to persuade Elizabeth into marriage or the choice of a successor there is evidence of collaboration, not only between the two Houses but also between noble patrons and their clients in the Commons.

M. A. R. Graves, **The Tudor Parliaments, Crown, Lords and Commons 1485–1603** (Longman, 1985)

Most government legislation put before Parliament was passed without delay. Discontent surfaced only over the most contentious issues such as Elizabeth's succession and marriage. Even then, Privy Councillors often 'primed' Parliament to discuss these issues as an extension of Privy Council business. For example, William Cecil lay behind persuading Parliament to discuss the marriage question. But Elizabeth ostracised him for six months.

◢ Source 10

The session of 1566–7 exemplified this. Once again the Queen required financial aid and the Council persuaded her to it. This was no mere cynical political exercise on the Council's part; the need was genuine enough. Nevertheless Councillors had bows with more than one string. When Parliament was summoned in September 1566 Cecil chaired a council meeting at which he proposed they pressed Elizabeth to marry.

M. A. R. Graves, **The Tudor Parliaments, Crown, Lords and Commons 1485–1603** (Longman, 1985)

Neale placed undue emphasis on the use of subsidy bills as a weapon to wrest concessions from the monarchy. Two points must be made in this connection. Subsidies were not a new tactic and had been used by Lancastrian Parliaments in the century before Elizabeth. Furthermore, the subsidy grant was challenged only once during Elizabeth's Parliaments, in 1566, and the attempt failed.

Neale also argued that there was an organised faction within the House of Commons and that leading Puritans were at its heart. Neither of these conclusions appears to be correct. There were always some politicians who thought differently from the Queen on some matters, but these men never formed an organised opposition, nor could they have done so because of the intermittent nature of Parliaments. Indeed, many of the Puritans supported the Anglican establishment although they wished to press for further reforms within its framework. They did not, however, represent a consistent and homogeneous group:

◢ Source 11

By careful analysis of the correspondence, their parliamentary drafts, and especially their role in committees and debates, Michael Graves [historian] has discovered that Thomas Norton, William Fleetwood, Thomas Dannett, Thomas Digges, Robert Bell, and others were not leaders of an organised opposition but agents of the [Privy] Council! ... These 'men of business' led the Commons into those issues which Councillors wanted discussed – which were often the issues Elizabeth wanted not to be discussed.

*C. Haigh, **Elizabeth I** (Macmillan, 1988)*

Thomas Digges was a client of Leicester, Thomas Dannett was Burghley's cousin, and James Dalton was a client of Burghley. Other so-called Puritan leaders were amongst Burghley's Parliamentary managers, particularly useful when Burghley was elevated to the House of Lords in 1571. Such individuals were vital to the smooth running of government, as was the informal network of kinship and patronage which existed at all levels of society. As Thomas Norton declared, 'All that I have done I did by commandment of the House and specially of the Queen's council there and my chiefest care was in all things to be directed by the Council.'

In any event Elizabeth could always put Parliament in its place. When Parliament had pressed the Queen to declare on the succession, she replied:

◢ Source 12

At this present it is not convenient, nor shall be without the some peril unto you, and certain danger to me. But as soon as there be a convenient time and that it may be done with least peril unto you, although never without great danger unto me, I will deal therein for your safety and offer it unto you as the prince and head without request. For it is monstrous that the feet should direct the head.

Extracts from the Queen's speech to the representatives of Parliament, November 1566

The 'political nation' (that section of the population – mainly the gentry and aristocracy – which, because of its wealth and privileges dominated political life at all levels of society) came closest to showing cracks in its edifice with the heated clashes over monopolies during the Parliaments of 1597–8 and 1601. Some monopolies were genuine and protected the copyright of the inventor. In trading monopolies the interests of the country as a whole were protected. Some were designed, however, solely to corner the market in a particular product and extort payment. Those who held monopolies enjoyed the support of the Privy Council and the Star Chamber and their opponents had little scope to resort to the law. In 1559 a bill to abolish monopoly licences vanished without trace in Parliamentary business. Robert Bell, a Privy Councillor, introduced a bill in 1571 to restrict the practice but withdrew it. By 1596–7 the number of monopolies had grown to such an extent that there was a renewed outcry against them. Some monopolies came under particularly savage attack. Sir Walter Raleigh had the monopoly in tin, playing cards and licences for taverns. Richard Norton attacked Raleigh's possession of monopolies on behalf 'of a country that groans under the burdens' laid on it by 'bloodsuckers of the Commonwealth'. A call for a committee of investigation was neutralised by Elizabeth who promised to review existing monopolies. The review did not happen. Indeed, new monopolies were created.

The 1601 Parliament was the most fractious. Robert Cecil did not manage Parliament as effectively as his father had done. He wanted a short Parliament and warned against 'fantastic speeches' and 'idle bills' and swiped at MPs who 'desired to be popular without the House for speaking against monopolies who also labour to be private within'.

Robert Wingfield was the most outspoken on the matter of monopolies in this Parliament and called on Elizabeth to 'take care of these monopolies', so that 'our griefs should be addressed'. Some wished to go further and introduce a bill. An outside demonstration brought Robert Cecil to the boil: 'Why, Parliamentary matters are ordinarily talked about in the streets! I have heard myself, being in my coach, these words spoken aloud "God prosper those that further the overthrow of these monopolies".'

Elizabeth, despite her advancing years, demonstrated her political skill once more by promising a review. Three days later a proclamation annulled twelve monopolies, enabled action against monopolies to be pursued through the courts and rescinded all letters of assistance from Privy Councillors in support of patentees. Monopolies were to remain a source of conflict and, in the hands of a monarch less politically shrewd than Elizabeth, a danger.

The Elizabethan Parliament, therefore, must be seen as the Queen in Council who guided business in both Houses through her Privy Council and its business managers. Only rarely was control lost. Even in these instances, the cause was usually to be traced to the Privy Councillors, covertly seeking to persuade Elizabeth to their opinion, or to factional interests, eager to seek advantage with the Queen. The very concept of 'opposition' had little meaning and 'Puritan opposition' even less.

The state of play among historians

The outbreak of the Civil War in the mid-seventeenth century between crown and Parliament has prompted many historians to search for the roots of the Civil War in the reign of Elizabeth. This may have led them astray, but as a student of this period you need to be aware of how this particular mindset has influenced historical interpretation. The Elizabethan Parliament was a working institution, dominated by the Queen in Council, who managed the business in both Houses and only rarely lost control. This apparent loss of control was most frequently the result of individual Councillors stirring up Parliamentary intrigues in order to further their own policy wishes, or of factional divisions. 'Opposition' as we understand the term in modern democratic government would have been an alien term and the notion of a 'Puritan opposition' even more misleading.

◢ Source 13

Whatever her reasons – an autocratic temper, a preference for secret politics, or a woman's defensive posture in a male-dominated world – she was not fond of Parliaments. Financial necessity and the Privy Council's prompting [often for other reasons] compelled her to call them. When she did she preferred short sessions and hustled Council, Commons, and Lords on to complete official business and so make an end of it.

M. A. R. Graves, **The Tudor Parliaments, Crown, Lords and Commons 1485–1603** (Longman, 1985)

◢ Source 14

Elizabeth adopted a tone of condescending superiority towards her Parliaments, confident that if she explained things often enough and slowly enough, the little boys would understand. For Elizabeth, Parliamentarians were little boys – sometimes unruly, usually a nuisance, and always a waste of an intelligent woman's time. Queen Elizabeth did not like Parliaments and it showed.

C. Haigh, **Elizabeth I** (Macmillan, 1988)

TASKS

1 Historians must always be alert to the fact that the terms we use today may have had substantially different meanings in the past. The subject of this chapter has been 'Parliament' and most of our understanding of the word will be derived from modern usage. How are Parliaments then and now similar and different?

Using the Venn diagram below, put the points you wish to make in the appropriate sector:

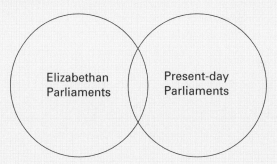

Elizabethan Parliaments

Present-day Parliaments

This simple device for organising information may help you to sort out your ideas when asked to provide a discussion or essay on similarities and differences.

2 The Queen had various devices for managing the affairs of Parliament. Read through the chapter and write them down.

When providing an explanation of *factors* it is necessary to *prioritise* i.e. to place the factors in order of importance. One device for doing this which may be helpful is as follows:

On separate strips of paper, write sentences on each principal method used by Elizabeth to control Parliament. Place the strips nearer or further from the question 'How did Elizabeth control Parliament?' *depending on how important you believe that factor to be*. If you think two or more factors are equally important, place them alongside each other.

3 Christopher Haigh claims that Elizabeth barely tolerated Parliaments and was reluctant to call them. Can this view be supported with reference to:

a their length and frequency?

b her official comments about Parliaments?

c her clashes with Parliaments?

d her reasons for summoning Parliaments?

e the gains, if any, that Parliament made during her reign?

4 There are predominantly two interpretations of the role of Puritans and the alleged growth in power of the House of Commons.
Set out the principal points as follows:

J. E. Neale argued that:	This has been disputed because:
◢	◢
◢	◢

5 Read the sources that follow:

◢ Source A

Mr Speaker, two things do very great hurt in this place of which I mean to speak. One is a rumour that runs about this House and it is 'take heed what you do, the Queen's majesty likes not such a matter; whoever prefers it, she will be much offended with him' ... The other is sometimes a message is brought into the House commanding or inhibiting, or injurious to the freedom of speech and consultation. I would to God, Mr Speaker, that these two were buried in Hell ... [God] did put it into the Queen Majesty's heart to refuse good and wholesome laws for her own preservation, which caused many faithful hearts for grief to burst out with sorrowful tears and moved all papists ... in their sleeves to laugh all the Parliament house to scorn ... none is without fault, no, not our noble Queen. Since then her Majesty has committed great faults, dangerous to herself and the state ... It is a dangerous thing in a prince unkindly to treat and abuse his or her nobility and people as her Majesty did in the last Parliament ...

> *Extracts from Peter Wentworth's speech in the House of Commons, 8 February 1576; quoted in I. Dawson, **The Tudor Century 1485–1603** (Nelson, 1993). Following this speech, Wentworth was expelled by the Commons and imprisoned by Elizabeth.*

a What complaints was Peter Wentworth making?

b Why did he consider the actions of Elizabeth to be dangerous to the state?

c Why were most MPs horrified at this speech? In what way were the sentiments expressed in this speech at variance with the Tudor concept of crown and Parliament?

◢ Source B

Mr Speaker,

We have heard your declaration and perceive your care of our estate. I assure you that there is no prince that loves her subjects better, or whose love can countervail our love. There is no jewel, be it of never so rich a price, which I set before this jewel; I mean your love. For I do esteem it more than any treasure or riches; for that we know how to prize, but love and thanks I count invaluable. And, though God hath raised me high, yet I count this the glory of my crown, that I have reigned with your loves. This makes me that I do not so much rejoice that God hath made me to be a Queen, as to be a Queen over so thankful a people. Therefore I have cause to wish nothing more than to content the subject and that is a duty which I owe. Neither do I desire to live longer than I may see your prosperity and that is my only desire. And as I am that person that still yet, under God, hath delivered you and so I trust by the almighty power of God that I shall be His instrument to preserve you from every peril, dishonour, shame, tyranny and oppression.

I have ever used to set the Last Judgement Day before mine eyes and so to rule as I shall be judged to answer before a higher judge, and now if my kingly bounties have been abused and my grants turned to the hurt of my people contrary to my will and meaning, and if any in authority under me have neglected or perverted what I have committed to them, I hope God will not lay their culps and offences in my charge. I know the title of a king is a glorious title, but assure yourself that the shining glory of princely authority hath not so dazzled our eyes of our understanding, but that we well know and remember that we are also to yield an account of our actions before the Great Judge. To be a King and wear a crown is a thing more glorious to them that see than it is pleasant to them that bear it. For myself I was never so much enticed with the glorious name of a King or royal authority of a Queen as delighted that God hath made me His instrument to maintain His truth and glory and to defend this kingdom as I have said from peril, dishonour, tyranny and oppression. There will never Queen sit in my seat with more zeal to my country, care to my subjects and that will sooner with willingness venture her life for your good and safety than myself. For it is my desire to live nor reign no longer than my life and reign shall be for your good. And though you have had, and may have, many princes more mighty and wise sitting in this seat, yet you never had or shall have any that will be more careful and loving.

Elizabeth's speech to Parliament, 1601 (often referred to as her 'golden speech')

a How does Elizabeth define herself as a ruler?
b From what power does she claim her authority?

c How does she explain the curbs on her power?

d How does Elizabeth display her skill as a speaker?

e Compare Sources A and B.

 i What differences are there in their interpretation of kingly power?

 ii What differences in tone are there between the two sources?

 iii The extract from Peter Wentworth's speech is a reaction against a particular piece of legislation. Elizabeth's speech is a general description of her belief in the attitude of the monarch to her people. How might this help in part to account for the differences?

 iv In what ways can the two speeches be said to represent the same attitude to monarchical power?

 v What examples of evidence would you require to support:
 ◢ Peter Wentworth's judgement?
 ◢ Elizabeth's judgement of herself?

6 *It has been argued that during the reign of Queen Elizabeth, the House of Commons gained in importance at the expense of both the House of Lords and the crown. How accurate is this statement to describe the changing relationship between crown and Parliament between 1559 and 1603?*

Use the following *writing frame* to help you structure your essay.

Parliament during the reign of Queen Elizabeth I, according to historians such as J. E. Neale ...

Recent research has suggested otherwise. The legal power of the monarch was such that ...

Parliament, however, had developed ...

Elizabeth was adept at managing her Parliaments by ...

The House of Lords remained more important than the House of Commons, for example, ...

The existence of a 'Puritan choir' has been disproved ...

Subsidy bills as weapons to gain advantage over the monarch ...

In conclusion, crown and Parliament were ... [the idea of the 'political nation']

CHAPTER THREE

FOREIGN POLICY – NATIONAL INTEREST OR PROTESTANT CRUSADE?

Objectives

⊿ To outline the course and analyse the direction of Elizabeth's foreign policies

⊿ To demonstrate the critical role of events in the Netherlands in determining Elizabeth's policy

⊿ To explain the fear of an alliance between the two major Catholic powers of Spain and France, and the measures taken to prevent an alliance

⊿ To explain the role of religious divisions in foreign policy.

The importance of the Netherlands

The elder statesman, Lord Paget, who had served in turn Henry VIII, Edward VI and Mary, was asked to sum up his years of experience of foreign relations in a memorandum to Elizabeth's Secretaries of State at the Queen's accession. Paget was in no doubt that France was the natural enemy of England and that Elizabeth's government needed to ensure a continuing friendship with the Habsburgs, who ruled over (among many other lands) the 17 provinces of the Netherlands.

The Netherlands played a crucial role in England's calculations for two reasons. Firstly, wool was England's main export, and the textile trade was centred on the great trading city of Antwerp. It was from the taxation on this commodity that the Queen obtained her greatest and most secure revenue. Secondly, whoever controlled the Netherlands had not only the means to stifle English trade but a springboard to launch an invasion against England. Economic and social stability for the crown and the people was therefore heavily dependent upon events in the Netherlands. Paget's conclusion was not lost on Elizabeth's Councillors.

It followed from England's position as a second-rate power that Elizabeth should seek an alliance with one of the two major powers – France or Spain – or, failing that, try to subvert any alliance between

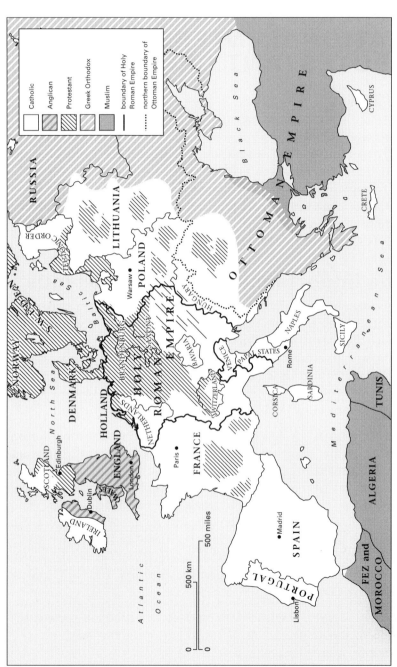

Figure 5 Religious and political divisions in Europe 1559

these two countries. A potential obstacle in the path of agreement with these powers was that they were both Catholic. Elizabeth would be placed in a very difficult situation at home if she was in alliance with a state that was suppressing Protestants. On the other hand, to aid her fellow believers would not only fracture diplomatic relations with these countries but could well drag her into costly commitments and wars.

International diplomacy

During the Middle Ages the infrequent despatch of a herald or messenger was virtually the sole means of international communication. By the sixteenth century this was no longer sufficient. Occasionally monarchs arranged diplomatic meetings and cultivated acquaintance through correspondence. Gradually the exchange of ambassadors had become normal practice. During the 1560s, French and Spanish diplomats were in residence at Elizabeth's court but the representative of the Holy Roman Emperor was withdrawn in 1560 and Venice failed to maintain an embassy in England. Few as these representatives were, they carried enormous responsibility.

Elizabeth maintained diplomats in France, Scotland and Spain, but surprisingly not in the Netherlands. This was mostly due to the makeshift and evolving nature of international representation. England's interests were represented there by the Queen's financial agent, Sir Thomas Gresham. Nevertheless, considering the critical role the Netherlands played in England's international strategy, this was a serious omission.

The Queen also made use of noblemen to accomplish specific diplomatic missions, as the Earl of Sussex did to Vienna in 1567, but there was no expectation that visits would be prolonged and nor did they receive a salary for their troubles. Nor were there many trained and experienced men who could accomplish these tasks, and Elizabeth was required to use a disparate group of individuals from the ex-Jesuit Dr Christopher Parkins to the secretary of the Merchant Adventurers at Antwerp. Foreign intelligence was normally collected by English merchants, co-ordinated by Cecil and from 1573 by Sir Francis Walsingham.

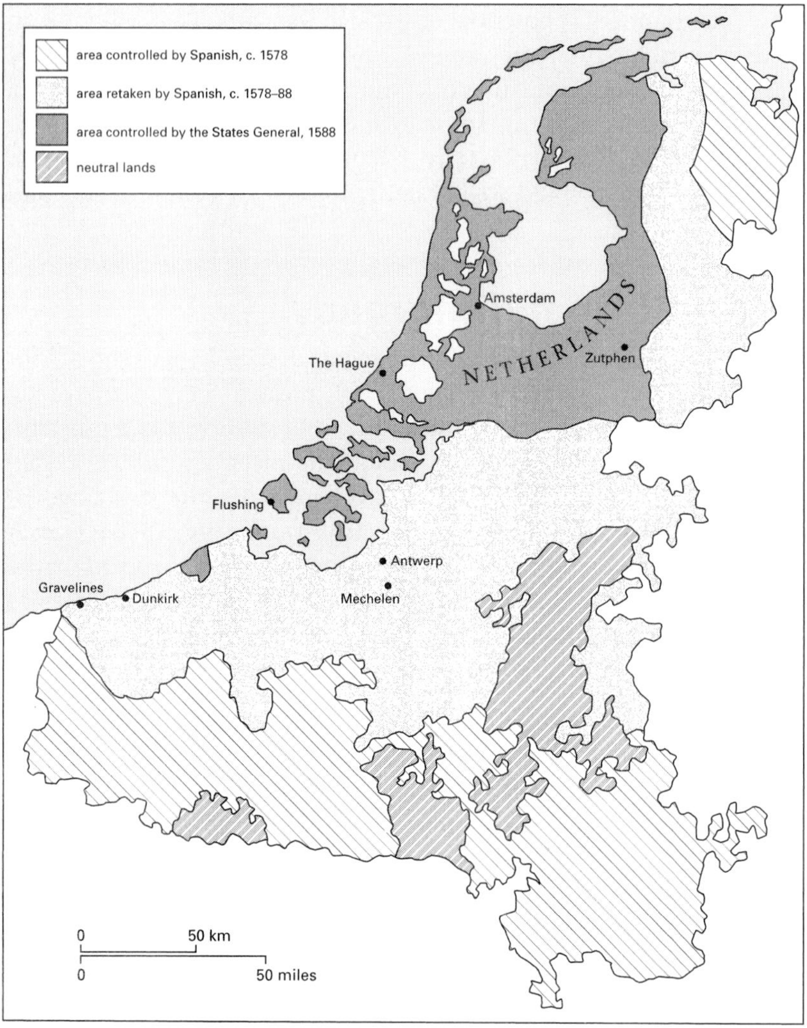
area controlled by Spanish, c. 1578
area retaken by Spanish, c. 1578–88
area controlled by the States General, 1588
neutral lands
Amsterdam
NETHERLANDS
The Hague
Zutphen
Flushing
Antwerp
Gravelines
Dunkirk
Mechelen
0
50 km
0
50 miles

Figure 6 The Netherlands

1558–62

Foreign policy during the opening years of Elizabeth's reign followed traditional lines. The situation, however, was complicated by the fact that Philip II had inherited the territories of the House of Habsburg and was therefore the ruler of the Netherlands provinces in addition to the kingdom of Spain and the vast expanses and riches of the recently discovered New World. However bitter the relationship became later, the signs for a cordial relationship looked promising at the beginning of Elizabeth's reign. Philip had been married to her half-sister Mary and had intervened on one occasion when Elizabeth's life had been in danger. Not long after Mary's death, Philip proposed marriage and although Elizabeth rejected the offer, she continued to rely on his support as the main buttress in her foreign relations for at least the first ten years of her reign. Indeed, she expressed regret that Philip left northern Europe within a year of his wife's death to return to Spain (which he never left during the remaining 40 years of his life).

The 'auld alliance' (France and Scotland)

The old antagonism with France was the first threat Elizabeth had to face. England was still at war with France at her accession, being dragged into the conflict as a result of its Burgundian alliance. The Treaty of Cateau-Cambrésis in April 1559 left Calais, the last English toehold in France, in French possession but with the face-saving formula that compensation would be paid and the town would be returned to England after eight years, providing peace was maintained. Calais, however, was destined never to be returned.

Relations between the two countries were not improved by the Treaty when the new King, Francis II, ascended the throne. His wife Mary, Queen of Scots and granddaughter of Margaret Tudor, assumed the title Queen of England. France used this as an opportunity to strengthen the 'auld alliance' between Scotland and England and was well placed to do so. Francis was only 15 years old, his wife 17. Effective power was in the hands of the powerful Guise family. The Duke of Guise's sister, also called Mary, was the mother of Mary Queen of Scots and Regent of Scotland, and was supported by a French garrison entrenched in Edinburgh Castle.

Elizabeth did not want to declare her hostility openly. Instead she undermined Mary of Guise's authority by sending secret supplies of money and materials in 1559 to a group of Scottish Protestant nobles called the Lords of the Congregation, who were in revolt against the French regent. William Cecil urged Elizabeth to send troops but she erred on the side of caution.

Her motives were that:

◢ she did not want to be seen as actively aiding rebels against a legitimate monarch
◢ if the English army failed in its purpose then French influence would increase
◢ defeat may tempt the French to invade
◢ she did not want to be accused of breaking the Treaty of Cateau-Cambrésis
◢ most importantly, she did not want to damage her relationship with Philip II.

If successful, however:

◢ the French presence would be removed from Scotland
◢ the Protestant lords in Scotland might assist the English in dominating Ulster
◢ a pro-English group would be established as the government in Scotland, forming a Protestant alliance
◢ Mary Queen of Scots' influence would be crippled, thus making it less likely that she could seriously challenge Elizabeth for the throne of England.

The need for action, however, determined events. In March 1560, having secured Philip II's agreement not to intervene, Elizabeth sent troops to besiege Leith, the port for Edinburgh, and a flotilla to intercept any possible French reinforcements. Other events also worked in her favour. France's ability to act in Scotland was undermined by a revolt of French Huguenots. Then Mary of Guise, the regent in Scotland, suddenly died and the fleet sent by the French was destroyed in a storm. In the summer of 1560, the French were dislodged from Edinburgh Castle and Cecil travelled north to negotiate the Treaty of Edinburgh. By the terms of the Treaty both sides agreed to withdraw their forces from Scotland, leaving the Scots free to fashion their own religion and government. Philip was prepared to accept, or at least ignore, the establishment of a Protestant government there, if it removed French forces from Scotland.

The action in Scotland summed up Elizabeth's principle dilemma. Although Protestant, she could not afford to base her foreign policy solely on assisting Protestants wherever the call might come from. Her first objective was national security and that meant an alliance with either France or Spain which, unfortunately from her point of view, were both Catholic.

In December 1560, events took a more threatening turn for Elizabeth, with the death of the young Francis II and the replacement by his brother Charles IX, who was firmly under the thumb of his mother, Catherine de Medici. Mary Queen of Scots no longer had a role in French affairs as far as Catherine was concerned and was shipped back to Scotland in the summer of 1561. The Scots queen was marooned, a Catholic monarch in a Protestant country, a product of French culture in a land that had rejected the French. Sensibly, she made no attempt to turn the tide of the Protestant Reformation. From Elizabeth's point of view, however, she and her main contender for the English crown now shared the same island.

1562–85

Despite Elizabeth's extreme reluctance to intervene in another country as a Protestant champion, she supported the French Huguenots in 1562–4 during the civil war. Although this ended in settlement, Anglo-French relations did not significantly improve. Elizabeth was conscious that she needed to keep France at a distance, particularly where Scotland and the Netherlands were concerned. On the other hand, as relations with Spain deteriorated she needed to come to an accommodation with France so as not to be opposed by two Catholic powers.

Circumstances, however, permitted England and France to agree the Treaty of Blois in 1572, a defensive agreement aimed at Spain. As there seemed little need for Elizabeth to pursue a marriage settlement with the Duke of Anjou, the French heir apparent, marriage negotiations were abandoned.

Such careful diplomacy came bloodily unstuck with the Guise-inspired St Bartholomew's Day massacre of 24–30 August 1572. Thousands of Huguenots were murdered at the instigation of Catherine. Neglecting Walsingham's advice to aid the Huguenots directly, Elizabeth decided to send assistance secretly so as not to upset the delicate agreement. At the same time she played the marriage card by conducting marriage negotiations with the Duke of Alençon, who belonged to the Guise's rival family. With Alençon's death in 1584, the diplomatic cards came tumbling down. Henry III, the Guise King of France, reached an accord with Spain. The Treaty of Joinville in 1584 brought Spain to the aid of Henry III in his struggle against Henry of Navarre, the Huguenot champion. Elizabeth now faced the opposition of both France and Spain.

Spanish antagonism, however, had the effect of stimulating England's search for alternative trading routes and markets. As Spain dominated many of the oceans of the world and the American continent, England's challenge to Spain's supremacy had the double benefit of weakening both Spain's military and economic power. English overseas enterprise had begun in the late fifteenth century and gathered pace from the 1550s onwards. John Willoughby and Richard Chancelor attempted to discover a new trade route to the East around the north-east of Europe in 1553. A little later Thomas Wyndham, William Towerson and John Lok explored the west coast of Africa, leading to Sir John Hawkins' and England's participation in the infamous slave trade. Sir Francis Drake is arguably the most famous of these explorers, motivated by the ambitions of a privateer and the destruction of Spanish monopoly of trade with the Americas. These voyages and raiding expeditions were crucial in laying the foundations of English seapower and her challenge to Spain from which developed an expansive empire.

From reluctant friend to reluctant foe

One thread runs through the first 30 years of Elizabeth's foreign policy – the transformation of the Habsburg connection from an ally into an implacable enemy. Elizabeth had taken elaborate precautions to avoid antagonising Philip but the closure of Antwerp to English merchants as a response to England's intervention in France had been the first warning shot. The excuses used by the Spanish had been the fear that English troops were infected with the plague and could carry it into Antwerp. At a stroke, English trade and the Queen's finances were jeopardised. Alternative markets were found in north Germany but when the Spanish discovered that the embargo was also harming them, trade was restored in 1565. Nevertheless, the repairs to the relationship were superficial and a number of factors plunged Spain and England into hostility once more:

⬧ The English ambassador to Philip II, Dr John Man, was expelled for an alleged misdemeanour. Elizabeth certainly regarded Man as being in the wrong. Unfortunately no replacement could be found and communication at this senior level was a serious omission.

⬧ The Spanish ambassador, Don Guerau de Spes, had little knowledge or experience of northern Europe and showed little diplomatic skill, referring to Cecil and Bacon as 'bare-faced heretics, pernicious and enemies to your majesty'.

⬧ In 1568 Sir John Hawkins' fleet had been seized by the Spaniards after he had put into port at San Juan de Ulua. The Spanish claimed a monopoly on all trade to their possessions in the New World and regarded Hawkins as little more than a privateer. Hawkins interpreted the incident as an attack on legitimate trading rights. Both sides felt aggrieved and the incident soured relations between the countries.

⬧ In 1567 the Duke of Alba was sent to the Netherlands to suppress revolt with a massive army under his command. In 1568 a Spanish fleet, loaded with bullion to pay for the troops in the Netherlands, sought shelter in English ports. De Spes, fearing that the treasure might be seized by Elizabeth, acted impulsively. He advised Alba to impound English ships and goods currently in the Netherlands as hostage for the release of Spanish treasure ships. Alba reluctantly did so. The reaction was predictable – Spanish goods and treasure in England were seized in retaliation. In 1569, trade between the two countries came to a halt and a hostile army was camped on the other side of the Channel.

The need for friends

This dramatic turnabout in international relations prompted Elizabeth to seek alternative alliances. Approaches to the north German princes for a Protestant confederation got nowhere and appeared less relevant as the tension eased between England and Spain. Sixteen years were to elapse before war actually broke out between the two countries but a series of incidents in that time propelled them, albeit reluctantly, towards open conflict. The Northern Rising in 1569 was followed by the Papal Bull of Excommunication of 1570 as well the papally-financed invasion of Ireland in 1579. Philip's malevolent presence was detected, with or without justification, behind the scenes.

Nor was the provocation all one-sided. English privateer raids on Spanish possessions and treasure ships grew bolder in the 1570s, and they did so with the knowledge and connivance of the Queen. Above all, the outbreak of revolt in the Netherlands in 1566, which steadily grew more serious after 1572, was the principal contributory factor in worsening relations. Despite the resumption of trade between England and Spain in 1573, relations had not been repaired and suspicion on the part of Spain exaggerated England's involvement in supporting the rebels. With no English envoy in Spain, little could be done to set the record straight.

A French alliance

The French noted with approval the deterioration in Anglo-Habsburg relations and revived the proposal of marrying one of Catherine de Medici's sons to Elizabeth. They were somewhat surprised to receive a favourable response, but owing to Elizabeth's skill at vacillation, the negotiations dragged on for 14 years until the death of the last surviving suitor in 1584. It was not only Elizabeth who was cynical about the prolonged discussions. The French, too, had much to gain from the increased prestige of their princes. The negotiations also provided Elizabeth with a legitimate means of interfering in French politics, particularly during the 1580s when civil war in France became a conflict over the crown. Elizabeth supported Henry of Navarre, the legitimate and Protestant claimant to the throne, whilst Philip II backed the Catholic League.

Elizabeth, however, could not claim she was backing the legitimate claimant in the case of the northernmost provinces of the Netherlands, where the States General formally rejected the sovereignty of Philip. In 1572 she had surreptitiously supported the rebels with supplies of arms and ammunition and from 1576 was lending substantial sums of money to the States General to maintain the resistance to Spain. The Treaty of Nonsuch in 1585 strengthened this relationship and the sending of Robert Dudley, Earl of Leicester as commander of an expeditionary force confirmed her personal support for their cause. Sensibly, she always maintained her distance from the conflict so as to provide her with the option of withdrawal should the occasion demand. This was typified in her refusal of the offer of sovereignty made by the States General. To have accepted the offer would have been to accept an unlimited obligation to defend her 'new' territories.

Her objectives, as always, were limited:

▲ to prevent the establishment of an enemy base in the Netherlands which could be used as a platform for the invasion of England

▲ to restore the Habsburg estate but to ensure that it was dominated by neither France nor Spain.

The reversal of alliances was not the sole result of England's foreign policy. The closure of Antwerp to English trade obliged merchants to look for alternative ports. Emden was chosen initially but was still too close to the Netherlands and hence to intervention. Hamburg provided a far safer opportunity. As a result, from 1569 onwards, English Merchant Adventurers, escorted by royal warships, sailed for this destination. There were disadvantages. Antwerp was the terminus for oriental spices and drugs and the luxury textiles of Italy. This state of affairs encouraged Italian merchants living in England to open direct trade links with their own country, encouraged not surprisingly by England. The Levant Company, founded in 1581, was chartered by Elizabeth to open Mediterranean trade to England and also to establish an English representative to the Sultan at Constantinople.

Mary Queen of Scots

Whilst Mary remained Queen of Scotland she represented a constant danger to Elizabeth, not only as a challenge to the English crown but also because of her French connection. With Mary's flight from Scotland and imprisonment by Elizabeth the threat was transferred from fear of French intervention to a succession of assassination plots hatched by a minority of English gentry but backed by Spain. From 1580 onwards, relations between Spain and England rapidly deteriorated:

▲ Philip inherited the kingdom of Portugal along with its vast territories in the New World and a massive fleet.

▲ In the Netherlands the Duke of Parma was making considerable progress in defeating the rebels.

▲ The Throckmorton Plot in 1583 had been uncovered. The conspirators planned to assassinate Elizabeth and replace her with Mary Queen of Scots. Spain had assisted in the plan.

▲ William of Orange, who had led the most effective opposition against the Spanish in the Netherlands, was assassinated in 1584.

1585–1603

In 1585 Elizabeth felt forced into a war she had tried long to avoid but events in the Netherlands at this time appeared to be precarious for the rebels. If defeated, their collapse would present England with considerable dangers from a Spanish invasion. The Treaty of Nonsuch promised military aid to the Dutch rebels and the Earl of Leicester led the reinforcements. England's intervention in the Netherlands was effective and by August 1586 the town of Zutphen (see map on page 88) had been captured. Although Leicester was successful on the battlefield the same could not be said of his diplomacy, which merely resulted in stirring up factions within the warring rebels. The Dutch also suspected, correctly as it happened, that the English were engaged in peace talks with Spain. Leicester resigned his commission in 1587 but English support for the Dutch continued, if less whole-heartedly.

The war with Spain was to last until 1604, with invasion attempts by Spain in 1588, 1596 and 1597 and a further one planned in 1599. A combination of English attacks and storms removed each threat. The wars were costly and imposed considerable strains on England's finances. Between 1589 and 1595 Elizabeth sent 8,000 troops to fight in the Netherlands and 20,000 to France. In addition, she gave £300,000 in aid to Henry of Navarre and £750,000 to the Dutch. It was little wonder that the Queen had increasing recourse to Parliamentary double and triple subsidies, for her ordinary revenue was little more than £250,000. Nevertheless there was much for Elizabeth to be jubilant about. In 1595, Henry of Navarre became King of France, although he was to exchange his Protestantism for Catholicism to reconcile the majority of his countrymen to his rule; as he explained, 'Paris is well worth a mass.' Even Philip's vast resources could not secure the Netherlands and under the leadership of Maurice of Nassau, the northern provinces saw their independence acknowledged in all but name by Spain (official recognition came in 1609). The southern Netherlands, however, remained under Spanish rule. This, too, was pleasing to Elizabeth for it provided a Spanish fortress against French expansionism. The war ground to a halt in 1604, largely because Philip's resources were seriously depleted and France had resumed her enmity with Spain.

Conclusion

Whilst the objectives of foreign policy, as they emerged over a period of time, were achieved, the cost was enormous. During the mid-1590s four successive poor harvests added to the distress. Food prices rose steeply – 35 per cent in the 1590s – and war added further fuel to inflation levels. Most people chose to blame the war rather than the poor harvests and the Queen and her Councillors as the instruments of their depression. Taxes mounted to pay for the subsidies. In 1559–71 the tax yield had been £690,000; in 1576–87 £660,000; in 1589–1601 £1,100,000. This was not the only burden: each county had to fund its own militia and raise troops for overseas service. The administrative duties of unpaid JPs multiplied.

Merchants, too, saw their profits affected, with the disruption of trade with the Netherlands initially and later with Spain itself. Whilst new markets were found, particularly beyond Europe, they did not prevent dislocation and hardship in the short term.

Elizabeth's objectives in foreign policy were always limited and practical. With the collapse of the Antwerp dependency, the Queen and her merchants were obliged to pursue an understanding with France and reluctantly to support the rebels in the Netherlands to prevent the domination of north-western Europe by England's principal enemy, Spain. English merchants were thus obliged to search out new markets around the Baltic and in the Mediterranean. Elizabeth always kept the importance of the cloth trade in her sights for this was also the main source of her revenue from foreign trade. Elizabeth's success in this respect can be judged by the survival of the cloth trade, her solvency and the defeat of the Armada in 1588. Despite the limitations of her foreign policy, England had survived several invasion attempts and overcome commercial crises.

These factors, along with the controversy over monopolies (see Chapter 2), did much to give the impression that Elizabeth's reign was sliding into ruin. Ironically, the Queen herself, the very person who had attempted to restrict England's involvement in European conflicts was blamed for this malaise.

TASKS

Turning points

Explaining turning points in history is of crucial importance, whether they be significant events or simply a point in time when a reversal of existing policy is clearly discernible.

1 In pairs, make a flowchart to illustrate Elizabeth's foreign policy. Underline those events you consider to be key. Develop an argument to justify your choice. If you find this difficult, restrict your choice to three events only.

2 Other student pairs may well have picked different events which they consider to be turning points. Listen to their arguments. Do you agree with the points they make or can you detect weaknesses in their justifications?

3 The historian G. D. Ramsay in 'The foreign policy of Elizabeth I' (in C. Haigh (ed.), *The Reign of Elizabeth I*, Macmillan, 1984) states: 'The central issues in international politics for over half the reign hung on the transformation of the Burgundian ally into a reluctant enemy.' Do you agree with this statement?
If so, decide which events might have contributed to this conclusion. What might Ramsay have meant by transforming the Burgundian ally into a '<u>reluctant</u> enemy'?

4 **Testing ideas with evidence**
You have had your ideas tested by others and in turn you have tested other people's interpretations of key events. Here are some statements which refer to Elizabeth's foreign policy. Find evidence to support/ oppose the statements. Then decide what your final verdict will be. Remember it's not the *number* of arguments that will determine your judgement but the *quality and significance* of the evidence.

   a 'Elizabeth provided a beacon for Protestant causes throughout Europe, actively supporting her co-religionists in men and money.'
   b 'Elizabeth always thought of national security first and all other considerations played a secondary role.'

c 'The fate of the Netherlands is pivotal in understanding the main direction of England's foreign policy.'

d 'Declaring war on Spain was a defeat for Elizabeth's policy.'

5 Playing power politics

As a member of Elizabeth's Privy Council, review the situation for aiding the Netherlands. What advice would you give Elizabeth? How might this advice differ depending on whether you are William Cecil or Robert Dudley?

Reasons to support the Netherlands:

- the Netherlands could be united as one single state
- support could be given to fellow-Protestants
- Elizabeth would win prestige amongst the Protestant powers of north Germany
- England was on friendly terms with France
- Spain was achieving little success in its suppression of the revolt.

Reasons not to support the Netherlands:

- the cost of aiding the Netherlands would be enormous because the power and resources of Spain would make any campaign protracted
- the rebels were managing to keep the Spanish in check without assistance
- if Spain were defeated then France might step in and dominate
- any support by England might be seen as a crusade against Catholicism and this might unite Catholic powers against England.

CHAPTER FOUR

POVERTY AND LEGISLATION – SOCIAL CONCERN OR SOCIAL CONTROL?

Objectives

◢ To understand why poverty increased during the reign of Elizabeth

◢ To understand why poverty began to be perceived as a social problem

◢ To review the range of legislation passed to deal with poverty

◢ To evaluate the success of the legislation in coping with poverty.

The background

The Poor Law legislation enacted by Elizabeth's Parliaments lasted without significant alteration until 1834, when many of its underlying principles were reasserted in the Poor Law Amendment Act of that year. It was not merely important in subsequent years but also during Elizabeth's reign itself. A succession of acts was passed in 1563, 1572, 1576 and 1598 and these were finally codified in 1601. The acts were designed to regulate the relief of the poor and control the activities of rogues and vagabonds. The poor, of course, had always existed, but during the reign of Elizabeth this area of social welfare and regulation was of increasing concern.

Was there really a problem?

Contemporaries were in no doubt that social dislocation was on the increase. Several explanations were put forward.

◢ Source 1

It is not yet full threescore years since this trade [begging] began, but how it hath prospered since that time it is easy to judge, for they are now supposed, of one sex and another, to account unto above 10,000 persons as I have reported.

*William Harrison, **The Description of England** (1586); edited by G. Edelen (Cornell University Press, 1968)*

◢ Source 2

The ruffler [mugger] hath served in many wars, or else he hath been a serving man; and, weary of well-doing, shaking off all pain, doth choose for himself this idle life and wretchedly wanders about the most shires of this realm.

> Thomas Harman, **A Caveat for Common Cursetors** *(London, 1567–73); quoted in E. Viles and F. J. Furnivall (eds),* **The Rogues and Vagabonds of Shakespeare's Youth** *(New Shakespeare Society, 1880)*

◢ Source 3

1597. On Saturday the 5th day of November the House [of Commons] met about eight o'clock in the morning;

Mr Francis Bacon spoke first and made a motion against enclosures and depopulation of towns and houses of husbandry and tillage. And to this purpose he brought in, as he termed it, two bills not drawn with a polished pen but a polished heart …

For enclosure of grounds brings depopulation, which brings first idleness, secondly decay of tillage, thirdly subversion of houses, and decay of charity, and charges to the poor, fourthly impoverishing the state of the Realm.

> Simonds D'Ewes (ed.), **The Journals of all the Parliaments during the reign of Queen Elizabeth**, *revised and published by Paul Bowes (1682)*

◢ Source 4

Whereas in times past we had sugar for four pence that now, at the writing of this treatise, is well worth half-a-crown, raisins or currants for a penny that now are holden at six pence, and sometimes at eight pence and ten pence the pound, nutmegs at two pence the ounce, ginger at a penny an ounce.

> William Harrison, **The Description of England** *(1586); edited by G. Edelen (Cornell University Press, 1968)*

◢ Source 5

That the number of our people is multiplied, it is both demonstrable to the eye and evident in reason, considering on the one side that nowadays not only young folks of all sorts but churchmen also of each degree do marry and multiply at liberty, which was not wont to be, and on the other side that we have not, God be thanked, be touched with any extreme mortality, either by sword or sickness, that might abate the overgrown number of us. And if in all, then in each sort, and in them the poorer sort also, must needs be augmented.

William Lambarde, 'An Ephemeris' in Conyers Read (ed.), **William Lambarde and Local Government** (Cornell University Press, 1962)

(There were three severe famines after this was written.)

In summary, contemporaries identified the following reasons as causes of poverty and vagabondage:

◢ men discharged from the wars seeking an idle life
◢ fewer agricultural labourers needed because of an increase of enclosures for sheep at the expense of arable land
◢ a rapid rise in prices which did not keep pace with wages
◢ increase in population adding a further strain on the food supply.

Historian's views

Historians generally agree on these factors but disagree over their scale and rate of change. Historians must take into account not merely the relative significance of these factors but also whether society and government perceived them as problems and why they felt legislation was necessary.

◢ Source 6

Pauperism was the result of many factors – rising population, conversion of arable to pasture, enclosure of common lands, racking of rents, growing dependence of industrial producers on overseas markets.

Christopher Hill, **Society and Puritanism in Pre-Revolutionary England** (Oxford, 1964)

◢ Source 7

Perhaps the least inadequate general index of prices is that devised by Professor Phelps Brown and Dr Hopkins, which is based on the cost of items in the hypothetical weekly budget of a building labourer in southern England. If prices in 1510 are taken as 100, they had risen by 1521 to 167. The index drops slightly to 150 in the early 1540s, and then rises to over 200 in the later 1540s and to 270 in 1555, 370 in 1556 and 409 in 1557, dropping suddenly to 230 in 1558. Since many people were living on a subsistence level in good years, it is not surprising that the late 1550s produced an exceptionally high death rate and unpopular governments. In 1597, a year of disastrously bad harvests, the index rose 180 points in one year to a peak of 685, and finally settled down in the early seventeenth century in the area of above 500.

Quoted in I. Dawson, **The Tudor Century 1485–1603** (Nelson, 1993)

◢ Source 8

The quality of harvests during the reign of Elizabeth (source: I. Dawson, *The Tudor Century 1485–1603*, Nelson, 1993)

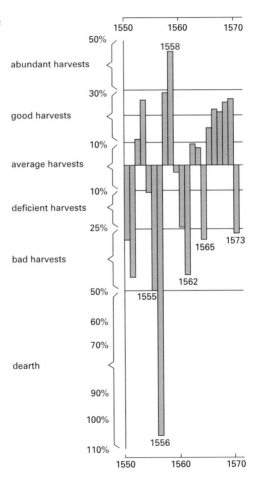

◢ Source 9

The purchasing power of wage rates

100 = value 1450–99

	Agricultural labourer	Building craftsman	London building worker
1540–9	71	70	76
1550–9	59	51	72
1560–9	66	62	82
1570–9	69	64	81

The rate of inflation 1540–79 (these figures use 1450–99 as the base (= 100). Source 7 referred to 1510 as the base) (source: I. Dawson, *The Tudor Century 1485–1603*, Nelson, 1993)

◢ Source 10

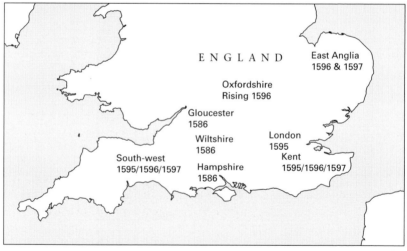

Rural disturbances in Elizabeth's reign

The weight of evidence suggests that the latter part of Elizabeth's reign was a time of increasing hardship for the majority of people. Earlier and more stable conditions had the effect of exacerbating the impact of rapid inflation and disastrous harvests. In their wake rural disturbances spilled into violence and threats to the regime.

None of these factors was particularly new despite their seriousness. We must turn our attention to the prescriptions of the Poor Law to appreciate how the government perceived the nature of the problem.

Early legislation

Many of the features of Elizabethan legislation to counteract poverty and vagrancy owed a debt to earlier legislation. Compulsory taxes had been imposed in most of the larger towns – London, York, Norwich in the late 1540s and 1550s. Although the taxes were initially temporary expedients, in many towns they became an established part of social regulation, for example in Chester, Cambridge and Exeter. Houses of Correction, such as the London Bridewell, also existed before national legislation was enacted.

◢ Source 11

… [there] shall be appointed a working place, as well as for men and women viz for the men to be prepared fourteen malt querns to grind malt and such exercises. And for the women to spin and card and such like exercises.

Which working place shall contain to set twelve persons or more upon work which persons shall be kept as prisoners to work for meat and drink for the space of twenty and one days at the least and longer if cause serve and they shall not eat but as they can earn.

Which persons shall begin their works at five o'clock in summer viz from Our Lady of the Annunciation until Michaelmas and shall end their works at eight of the clock at night, and in winter to begin at six of the clock from Michaelmas to Our Lady, and to end at seven of the clock at night.

And those that refuse to do their works to them appointed or keep their hours to be punished by the whip.

The Mayors Book for the Poor: Orders for the
Poor 1571 in Hudson Records of Norwich

Whilst local initiatives set the precedents for national legislation the government had also been particularly proactive. For example, a major

Elizabethan innovation was the Book of Orders which was distributed to all JPs and was intended to produce conformity of practice. The Book of Orders gave instruction on:

- famine – JPs were required to carry out surveys of grain when the harvests were meagre and to ensure there was a fair distribution to the poor
- plague – infected houses were to be quarantined and the sick were to be supported and prevented from infecting anyone else.

The Book of Orders was not an isolated example of Elizabethan concern for social issues. Regulations governing the growth and development of London were attempted, although with little success, by means of statutes in 1580 and 1593. In the countryside, regulations were passed to prevent the building of cottages on commons and wastes and the statutes of 1563 and 1598 were directed against further enclosure for pasture. Attempts were made to regulate wage labour by the Statute of Apprentices 1563.

Again, there was nothing particularly new in the subject matter of these statutes but there was a change in emphasis.

Source 12

Some old concerns fell into the background and others came to the fore. If we look at proclamations concerning vagrants, for example, it is notable that six of the nine Elizabethan proclamations on apparel were issued before 1581, while ten out of thirteen proclamations concerning vagrancy were issued after 1581. Parliamentary interest in the condition and conduct of the poor also increased in the last two decades of the reign ... poverty, on which there were at least seventeen bills in the 1597–8 session alone: drunkenness, inns and alehouses, on which there were thirteen bills between 1576 and 1601; profanation of the Sabbath, giving rise to six bills between 1584 and 1601; and bastardy and swearing, on which there were bills in 1597 and 1601 respectively. The manners and behaviour of the lower orders rather than of their betters seemed urgently to require reformation at the end of the reign.

Paul Slack, 'Poverty and Social Regulation in England' in C. Haigh (ed.),
The Reign of Elizabeth I *(Macmillan, 1984)*

Concerns for regulation of the poor were mirrored by local bye-laws governing control of lodging houses, restrictions on the subdivision of houses, the number of alehouses and so on. The amount of social regulatory activity revealed the ruling authority's preoccupation with increasing pauperism and vagrancy.

The 1601 Poor Law

The Poor Law of 1601 codified previous legislation and had three important features:

- A compulsory poor rate was laid on each parish and provided the resources for poor relief. By the Act of 1563 penalties could be imposed on those who refused to pay. In 1572, JPs were enabled to determine the size of the contribution. This power was transferred to the overseers of the poor in 1598.

- Begging was prohibited unless licensed by the authority. Penalties for vagrancy became increasingly harsh. By the Act of 1598, a beggar could be whipped on the authority of the parish and returned to his or her original parish.

- An effort to provide work for the destitute so they had little excuse or reason to leave the parish or claim relief without some labour. The Act of 1576 enabled JPs to provide parishes with flax or similar materials and a House of Correction for those who refused to work. Few parishes took advantage of this act and those that did tended to operate the system on a limited basis.

Were the views of contemporaries justified?

Specific political events, such as the Northern Rising of 1569, rather than an analysis of general economic trends, fuelled the ruling classes' sense of social instability. Whilst vagabondage was not the cause of the Northern Rising, it was widely believed that it could contribute to such political instability. In a number of areas of the country, social welfare schemes were remodelled after political upheaval, for example in Bristol, London and Norwich.

The last two decades of the sixteenth century were particularly difficult. Plague spread to many towns and threw people on poor relief as did the harvest failures of 1586, 1595, 1596 and 1597. Most disturbing to the ruling classes was the fact that social distress brought an increase in crime.

◢ **Source 13**

Indictments for capital felonies in Middlesex			
	%	Theft	Homicide	Assault and riot
1591	72	63	3	11
1592	126	118	5	5
1593	43	39	4	3
1594	65	57	3	6
1595	89	87	1	4
1596	69	68	1	10
1597	168	159	7	13
1598	258	239	18	43
1599	126	112	11	29

Indictments for capital felonies, 1591–9

Were conditions deteriorating in the longer term?

Whilst the 1598 and 1601 legislation was clearly an indication of economic crises it is less certain whether it was also indicative of longer-term decline. Population rose faster than the creation of jobs; prices faster than wages. The Phelps Brown and Hopkins indices (page 102) show that wages fell by 25 per cent in real terms during Elizabeth's reign.

Nevertheless, it is possible to see why Parliament legislated against vagrancy, against squatters on common and waste land and against the uncontrolled growth of London. A rising population was aggravating the problem of poverty and producing the context for social and political instability. Although the evidence is incomplete, there are some strong indications that there were more cases of punishments meted out to vagrants in the later part of Elizabeth's reign. In 1598, 67 vagrants were punished compared to the usual six or seven; in Salisbury 96 compared to fewer than 20. London, as might be expected, sky-rocketed from 69 in 1560–1 to 209 in 1578–9 and to 555 in 1600–01. Furthermore, vagrancy soon came to be the principal felony, up from about 16 per cent of cases in the 1560s to 62 per cent in 1601.

At the same time it is essential to understand that the prosecutors made little distinction as to the cause of the crime. Many of the wandering poor did turn to petty crime but vagrancy covered anyone who had no visible means of support, including the lame and the blind. Many had been servants or had had trades. What is now clear is that the economy could not easily absorb this increase in population, but contemporaries saw the solution in much more relatively simple terms: drive out those poor who did not belong to the parish and provide work and Houses of Correction for the rest. In truth, the idle probably constituted a small percentage of the total of poor (between 12 per cent and 16 per cent) while the vast majority were claimants through disability or unemployment. In Norwich, for example:

◢ Source 14

Causes of poverty in Norwich, 1598

35%   old age
7%   desertion by the father
8%   too large a family
50%   irregular employment or employment on low wages

*Quoted in I. Dawson, **The Tudor Century 1485–1603** (Nelson, 1993)*

A similar picture emerges in the countryside at the same time. By the end of Elizabeth's reign the authorities in three north Kent parishes were increasingly obliged to provide for labourers and their families alongside the usual powerless poor.

Was social regulation a matter for government?

The main thrust of government regulation was social control: to maintain things as they were. At the same time the debates that ensued contained the seeds for radical government intervention.

There were those who vehemently opposed the Poor Laws, first and foremost because they involved taxation. Others objected because they saw the law being used to persecute the poor further, as a Thetford man in 1577 observed, 'dealing with the poor but not with the rich'.

There were also matters of principle that lay behind these debates which echo down to our own age. The first was whether the government should intervene at all in matters which might be better left to charity. The parishioners of the West Riding of Yorkshire demonstrated this attitude when they refused to implement the laws against begging and the imposition of rates in 1598, contending 'many are able to give relief in kind but are not able to give money'. The second related question was how much flexibility should be allowed in the giving of relief.

Views were not clearly articulated on the matter, and principle as well as practice was much confused and largely pragmatic. Beggars still called at the rich man's house for alms and even when the practice of poor rates became more widespread after 1598, the sums raised probably never equalled those raised privately. This was, however, not the perception of many people living at the time.

◢ Source 15

... considering your most tender, pitiful, gentle, and noble nature – not only having a vigilant and merciful eye to your poor, indigent and feeble parishioners; yea, not only in the parish where your honour most happily doth dwell, but also in others nearby ... abundantly pouring out your ardent and bountiful charity upon all such as come for relief unto your gates ...

Epistle to Lady Elizabeth, Countess of Shrewsbury, in Thomas Harman, **A Caveat for Common Cursetors** *(London, 1567–73); quoted in E. Viles and F. J. Furnivall (eds),* **The Rogues and Vagabonds of Shakespeare's Youth** *(New Shakespeare Society, 1880)*

Nevertheless, the trend was towards greater government intervention and social regulation. This may well have been due to the belief that the old practices had singularly failed to solve the problems. W. K. Jordan (*Philanthropy in England 1480–1660*, 1959; Greenwood Press, 1978), suggests otherwise. He claims that charities remained particularly significant in supporting the destitute and had adequately compensated for the loss of monastic contributions. Contemporaries, however, witnessed more tangible evidence, such as the disappearance of poor boxes in churches.

Governments, too, were increasingly keen to demonstrate their humanitarian concern for the less fortunate, sometimes influenced by religious impulse, sometimes by the desire for maintaining social stability. William Cecil's encouragement of the projects in the Book of Orders is an example of his interest in economic and social matters.

Local JPs were also infected by the bureaucratic urge to develop and extend their jurisdiction over the neighbourhood and to be suspicious of vagrants as potential criminals.

◢ Source 16

... order is to be given in market towns and other places, that all suspected passengers, vagabonds, beggars, and rogues be punished with severity and celerity, according to the late statute.

State Papers, Domestic *1566–1579*

Protestant religious impulses may also have played an important role in stimulating the social conscience. R. H. Tawney's *Religion and the Rise of Capitalism* (1926; Penguin, 1990) describes the Puritan ethic on social issues as one of harsh retribution towards those who had failed to provide for themselves. Tawney was keen to develop his thesis that Protestantism was inextricably linked with the development of a capitalist and individualised work ethic and this may have led him to this exaggerated conclusion. Recent research suggests that Puritans were no different from other sections of society and that they discriminated between the causes of poverty as did others. That aside, there is considerable evidence that Puritans, in their desire to produce a godly society, were active in promoting beneficial projects. The minister and the magistrate frequently went hand in hand on these issues. Thomas Cartwright, a Protestant preacher, assisted in producing the listings of the poor in Warwick in the 1580s which not only increased alms for the poor but also encouraged greater opportunity for distributing funds on a discriminatory basis. Similar outcomes occurred in Norwich under the Puritan mayor John Aldrich (1570–2). Many other examples can be found. In Parliament the Puritans Wroth and More were active on committees on a wide range of issues concerning the lower orders. These displays of paternalistic concern were bound to spill over into a desire to reform the idle and the dissolute and it was not surprising that once this group was targeted, even the deserving poor were regarded with suspicion. It also led to some individuals putting particular 'spins' on all poor by their association with the dissolute poor. This affected contemporary thinking about the scale of the problem and produced what Professor

Patrick Collinson in *The Religion of Protestants. The Church in English Society 1559–1625* (OUP, 1982) calls 'collective paranoia'.

What effect did poor relief have?

In the absence of any significant redistribution of wealth from the rich to the poor the overall effect of poor relief was minimal. J. F. Hadwin ('Deflating Philanthropy', in *Economic History Review*, 1978), demonstrates that less than 0.25 per cent of national income came from endowed charities. Public measures, such as subsidised sales of grain, control of markets and increases in outdoor relief, probably had a greater effect. But such measures were reactive and palliative. They did not attack the causes of poverty and to have done so would have been tantamount to questioning the whole basis of social wealth and order.

◢ Source 17

The sticks as well as the carrots present in Elizabethan social policies thus helped to satisfy contemporary expectations and so to maintain social stability, even if the promise was greater than the performance in both cases. The ambivalent combination of charitable generosity and social discipline which we have seen in the vagrancy and poor-rate provisions of the law, in the ambitions of Puritan activists and in the efforts of local authorities, served a purpose. It was an uneasy combination, but regulation and relief, social control and provision for the poor went hand in hand – as in social policies they always do.

Paul Slack, 'Poverty and Social Regulation in England' in
*C. Haigh (ed.), **The Reign of Elizabeth I** (Macmillan, 1984)*

Famine and revolt

The food riots of the 1590s hardly suggest that welfare provisions were effective in maintaining social order. But grain distribution and outdoor relief funding may have had an effect on attitudes if not on realities. The poor may well have been persuaded that the government had their interests at heart and that the middlemen were responsible for the shortfalls. In this sense the government was attempting to restore balance to the social order. There were probably other reasons, too, associated with these social policies. As communities became increasingly polarised between rich and poor there was a change in attitude amongst the middling ranks who likewise became concerned at the potential disorder of the lower orders and sided with the ruling classes.

It is also important to distinguish those parts of the country that were affected by dearth. In 1596–7 the national death rate leapt to 21 per cent and in Cumbria there was actual starvation. Harvest failures hit hardest in upland regions where the margin of survival was more difficult. Richer agricultural regions to the south fared much better and London was provided with imported grain from the Baltic. The plague, on the other hand, affected the most densely packed areas.

Poor harvests had an impact on crime rates, although this tended to become manifest after a series of failures rather than immediately. Marriage rates declined whilst illegitimacy rates climbed. Whilst disorders occurred, they tended to be sporadic and with mainly short-term objectives. The government, with few public order resources at its disposal, tended to react with violence to ensure that the object lesson was not lost on any other potential troublemakers. This was illustrated by the government's response to the Oxfordshire rising in 1596. Only four rebels actually turned up to spark the rebellion and they were quickly arrested. The Privy Council showed no mercy and, after torture and confession, they were executed for 'levying war against the Queen' – a somewhat exaggerated description of their futile activities. No person of influence was tempted to participate in the rebellion, demonstrating that the middle yeomen had little sympathy for the labouring poor.

Despite the weakness of the Oxfordshire rising, the government was faced with real problems of social dislocation which reached crisis proportions in the last decade of Elizabeth's reign.

Summary

◢ Inflation represented a fundamental difficulty which war expenditure made worse.

◢ Population growth was not matched by increase in work opportunities and many people suffered poverty as a result of underemployment.

⬛ Enclosures, particularly in central and eastern England, reduced the numbers required for agricultural employment.

⬛ Trade slumps occasioned by falling demand and the uncertainties of the markets in the Netherlands created periodic unemployment.

⬛ Plagues, harvest failures and the return of discharged soldiers and sailors added to the pool of discontent.

Were the successes of Elizabeth's government overshadowed by the problems?

Despite the hardships of the last decade of Elizabeth's reign, a steadily rising birth rate was combined with an increase in life expectancy. Mortality rates were fierce in 1586–7 and 1594–8 but they were not national in extent. Additionally, starvation was averted in the south-east by the importing of grain from the Baltic region.

Nevertheless, the provisions of the Poor Laws must be seen as inadequate. The estimated cash yield of endowed charities for poor relief in 1600 totalled £11,776 per annum. This did not produce the widespread unrest that was feared for the Poor Laws operated as a palliative; they convinced the labouring poor that the ruling classes were on their side against the exploitative middlemen.

⬛ Source 18

Although Elizabethan government worked well until 1595, thereafter the strains of war, taxation and economic distress proved corrosive. In 1596 the Privy Council fell victim to moral panic, 'their own anxieties seemingly confirmed by the fantasies blown into their ears'. On the other hand, the governing class stood more united than ever before when faced by the mass of 'labouring poor', servants, and vagrants. Indeed, more meaningful than notions of a declining taxation system, corruption in central government, and an alleged 'slide to disaster' in the country is the idea of an expanding early modern state in which the powers of 'established authority' were growing at the expense of the population as a whole. But the solidarity of the propertied society ensured that the putrefying effects of war and court factionalism were muted before 1603.

C. Haigh (ed.), **The Reign of Elizabeth I** (Macmillan, 1984)

Explaining cause and effect

The most important question a historian can ask is, 'Why do things happen?' The first characteristic of an historian's approach to the problem of cause is that he or she will attempt to identify several causes for the same event. What may emerge from this consideration is a number of related but different types of causes – economic, political, ideological and personal. Some may have more significance in the short term whilst others may have developed over a longer period of time. The compulsion is then to order the factors in some form of hierarchy or priority determined by the nature of the enquiry. Decisions have to be made on a number of related issues:

a Is there sufficient evidence to support one cause as more important than another?

b In what ways are causes related to one another and how will they therefore be grouped?

c Are the causes conditional, i.e. setting the necessary preconditions for an event to take place? Or are they contingent, i.e. actual triggers for the event?

1 According to contemporaries, what were the main causes of poverty?

2 What reasons have historians given to explain the causes of poverty?

3 Arrange these causes in a hierarchy of importance.

4 Identify which causes are conditional and which are contingent.

5 Which causes are economic/political/ideological?

6 Repeat the list of questions, but this time focus on the reasons why government felt obliged to intervene.

Answering an enquiry

What were the causes of poverty in late Elizabethan England and why did the government intervene with legislation in 1598 and 1601 to deal with the problem?

A useful device for assembling and discussing the information to answer this enquiry is to group the principal causes around the central question or in this case, two questions. Brainstorm the causes of the following two questions and arrange them nearer or further away from each question, depending on their importance.

◢ What were the causes of poverty in late Elizabethan England?

◢ Why did the government intervene with legislation in 1598 and 1601 to deal with the problem?

Having decided a particular arrangement, discuss your conclusions with other students in your group/s. Change the order of your causes if you think you have heard convincing reasons for repositioning the arguments.

CHAPTER FIVE

GLORIANA – A GOLDEN AGE?

Elizabeth I ruled for almost 45 years. This book has presented you with a selection of some crucial themes of her reign – the Religious Settlement, foreign policy, her Parliaments, and legislation to control vagrancy and poverty. This is, of course, not the full story: that can be examined in some of the publications listed in Further Reading (page 124). It is now time to pass a verdict on the reign as a whole – the judgement is, of course, likely to be qualified for there will be little that can be regarded as wholly good or wholly bad. The verdict also depends upon where you place most emphasis: there is little doubt that if Elizabeth had died at the end of the 1580s the judgement of historians would have been more favourable.

The verdict of historians is also mixed. This chapter presents a selection of extracts from leading publications – remember these represent only a *selection* and many more books have been written on Elizabeth. No doubt she will prompt still more. Furthermore, only *extracts* are presented and it is important to read more widely to capture fully the different emphases that historians place at crucial points in their interpretations.

Lastly, it is important to consider what impact Elizabeth made as an individual upon events. Was she swept along by the current of the times? Would England have emerged as successfully from her foreign wars without her? Would an equally satisfactory Religious Settlement have been devised without her particular influence? Would government machinery have coped as adequately with the increasingly heavy demands made upon it?

The historical interpretation of Elizabethan political history has been subject to revisions.

By 1960 Sir John Neale dominated the field in three detailed studies which appeared to be the definitive word on the subject.

By the late 1970s, however, revisionist studies were beginning to filter through to question Neale's judgements. G. R. Elton led the criticisms, contesting Neale's interpretation that the seeds of Parliamentary and monarchical breakdown leading to the Civil War in the 1640s had been sown during the reign of Elizabeth. It must be stressed, though, that not all Neale's work should be jettisoned as flawed, for nothing could be further from the truth. As Christopher Haigh explains in *The Reign of Elizabeth I* (Macmillan, 1984), 'it is the fate of those who have dominated a subject to be attacked by those who come after – as it is the fate of those who stand on a giant's shoulders to be accused of trampling him down'. Controversy is the natural medium for the historian and only by debate and research can the subject retain its vitality and relevance.

◢ Source 1

Doubtless a tragic quiet [at the closing of Elizabeth's last Parliament] had fallen on the country, but, as this Parliament revealed, while Queen Elizabeth lived to set the hearts of people aflame, the spirit of her England was not dead. Even as members were arriving back in their homes, intoxicated with their Sovereign's golden words and her infinite graciousness and affection, Mountjoy in Ireland won an overwhelming victory … – one of the most decisive events in Irish history. It was a triumph that reflected credit on Sovereign as well as servant, for though the story of Essex in Ireland might suggest that Elizabeth was a difficult mistress to serve, her relations with Mountjoy showed that she could be helpful and inspiring where there was honest effort and a dutiful mind.

J. E. Neale, **Queen Elizabeth I** (Jonathan Cape, 1934)

◢ Source 2

Few rulers have impressed themselves so forcibly on the memory and imagination of the English race as Queen Elizabeth I. It may be admitted, of course, that much of the lustre surrounding her name is adventitious; that her reputation as Queen, like that of Louis XIV, lies bathed in the reflected glory of the people she governed. Even so, however, 'Elizabethan England' was, in a very real sense, Elizabeth's England. She it was who nursed it into being, and by her wisdom made possible its amazing development. Her characteristic virtues and defects, her sympathies and antipathies, her very whims and caprices are writ large across its political firmament. She inspired its patriotism, its pageantry, its heroisms, stimulated its poetry, and shaped its destiny. And when she died she left behind her a kingdom that had won a commanding position among the great powers of Europe.

J. B. Black, **The Reign of Elizabeth 1568–1603** (Clarendon Press, 1936)

Source 3

The reign of Elizabeth was not one of reform but of exploitation and consolidation. After the vast overhaul of the machinery which was part of [Thomas] Cromwell's achievement, what was needed was a little development but in the main use; and these the great Elizabethan administrators provided ... The sorting had been done under Henry VII and Henry VIII, and in particular by the genius of Tudor times, Thomas Cromwell; without the long labours, the years of drudgery, the high and honest endeavour of the Elizabethans no amount of revolutionary genius would have sufficed.

G. R. Elton, **England under the Tudors** (CUP, 1955)

Source 4

Overall it can be argued that the traditional picture of Elizabeth's reign as a great age for the Queen and the English nation contains much truth. But it is not the whole story. There are important elements of failure and of lost opportunities in the reign. Above all, perhaps, a more imaginative approach to the administration of the customs and the crown lands could have left the monarchy in a much happier financial position than the one which faced James I in 1603. Many of his worst troubles and those of his son, Charles I, stemmed from that unsatisfactory financial heritage.

A. G. R. Smith, 'The Reign of Queen Elizabeth I: An Assessment' in **History Sixth**, Volume 3; quoted in I. Dawson, **The Tudor Century 1485–1603** (Nelson, 1993)

Source 5

Whereas bouts of intense factionalism had divided courtiers and Councillors under Henry VIII with inevitable disruption to careers and government alike, the homogeneity of court and Privy Council under Elizabeth was a major source of stability. It has often been claimed that late Elizabethan government was inherently weak, and that 'corruption sapped the system's vitality' until 'it collapsed'. But there was no high road to the Civil War. If the breakdown of 1640–2 had a number of long-term causes, the vital dynamic was always Charles I's conduct and policies. ... if we read history backwards, Elizabeth's inertia and immobility in the 1590s, combined with the rise of 'venality' at court, could be said to have established a pattern that precluded comprehensive reform. Of course, no one would deny that Elizabeth's last years were tainted by the cumulative strain of a war economy, Irish affairs, Essex's revolt, and the harvest failures of 1594–7.

Yet history is properly read forwards. When this is done, it is clear that a 'slide to disaster' was inconceivable in the sixteenth century. Elizabeth controlled her own policy; the Privy Council was a tightly organised body; communications with the localities were good; a Protestant consensus had emerged. True, financial administration was not free from scandals, but Elizabeth left her successor a relatively small debt.

J. Guy, **Tudor England** (1949; OUP, 1990)

◢ Source 6

Elizabeth's success as a ruler was very much a personal triumph, for much of the devotion and loyalty she inspired was attributable not solely to her authority, but to her glamour, magnetism and charm. As her godson, Sir John Harrington, recalled, 'Her speech was such as none could refuse to take delight in ... When she smiled it was pure sunshine that everyone did choose to bask in if they could.' She combined remarkable talents as an orator with the surest of touches in dealing with individuals, and when she was out to please, she was well nigh irresistible ... It was true there was an obverse side to the Queen's character, for her temper was far from even, and she suffered from the fault of being 'too apt to wrath by the murmur of backbiters' ... Yet though it was naturally upsetting for her employees to be censured without good cause, they knew that if Elizabeth was in the wrong, she generally recognised the fact before too long, and proved anxious to make amends.

... the nation regained self-confidence and sense of direction ... she upheld the interests of the crown while not encroaching on those of her subjects, restored the coinage, and created a Church which, for all its failings, came close to being truly national. While many European countries were rent by civil war, insurrection and appalling acts of bloodshed, she presided over a realm which (with the exception of her Irish dominions) was fundamentally stable and united ... Besides this, Elizabeth was responsible for raising England's international standing, defying the most powerful nation in Christendom, and frustrating Philip II's attempts to overrun both England and France.

A. Somerset, **Elizabeth I** (Weidenfeld and Nicolson, 1991)

◢ Source 7

[Elizabeth] had to resist the machinations of her Councillors as they tried to draw her into their schemes. Her sources of intelligence were almost uniformly unreliable, and her own advisers and ambassadors, as well as foreign diplomats, fed her the

information which suited them. The specific policies (or tactics) she pursued had little positive support ... And she had to achieve all this despite an appalling political handicap; she was a woman in a man's world.

... Elizabeth had a restricted conception of her role as Queen. Though she spoke much of her duty to God and her care for her people, this was political rhetoric to justify her rule ... Elizabeth's objective as Queen was to be Queen; her exercise of royal power was not a means to a higher end, it was an end in itself.

In the new and bitter world of the 1590s, Elizabeth was shown to be politically bankrupt. The only answer she and those close to her could provide seemed to be 'more of the same'. For her political style, this meant more resort to ill temper as a tool of management, more reluctance to spend money on necessary policies, more reliance on and reward of a few trusted advisers. For her political image, this meant more extravagant praise of non-existent qualities, more far-fetched portrayals of idealised beauty, more frequent repetitions of the old slogans. The world in which Elizabeth had painstakingly built her model of female monarchy changed – but Elizabeth lived up to her motto, semper eadem, always the same. She was a ruler overtaken by events – 'a lady whom time had surprised', as Raleigh remarked.

C. Haigh (ed.), **The Reign of Elizabeth I** (Macmillan, 1984)

◢ Source 8

... On the whole, and with of course, a few notable exceptions, historians writing about her have been male ... There is a strain running through the work of even the most eminent historians that reveals an uneasiness about Elizabeth's sex. This is manifested most obviously in the way in which Elizabeth's tactics of vacillation and her constant changes of mind have been described pejoratively as quintessentially 'feminine' ... This it seems to me, is both over-simplistic and patronising. Elizabeth learned that to hold an inflexible position could mean death; ... This tactic [of delaying decision] worked so well in her youth that it must have been second nature. As monarch she continued to use it ... Rather than interpreting this character trait as quintessentially feminine, it is more useful to see it for what it was – a behavioural pattern learned in childhood and carried to extremes once she was out of immediate danger. It is the clue to Elizabeth's survival.

S. Basnett, **Elizabeth I: A Feminist Perspective** (1988); quoted in
I. Dawson, **The Tudor Century 1485–1603** (Nelson, 1993)

The judgement of historians

1 Read Sources 1, 2 and 3.

    a What does Neale mean when he says a 'tragic quiet' had fallen on the country? What do phrases such as this convey about Neale's attitude to Elizabeth and his judgement about her reign?

    b What events does Neale quote to support his view?

    c What events could be quoted that had occurred at this time which would cast doubt on Neale's judgement of the final years of Elizabeth's reign?

    d In what way does Black's interpretation differ from Neale's?

    e What conditional causes does Elton place upon the achievements claimed by Neale?

2 Read Sources 4 and 5.

    a What are the suggested links between Elizabeth's reign and the Civil War that broke out in the mid-seventeenth century?

    b Do these historians suggest that the links can be justified?

3 Read Source 6, and then 1 and 2 again.

    a What personal qualities does Somerset consider Elizabeth possessed which contributed to the success of her reign?

    b Almost 60 years separate Somerset's book from that of Neale. What conclusion is it possible to come to concerning the debates that have taken place about Elizabeth's qualities as a monarch?

4 Read Source 7.

    a What were Elizabeth's shortcomings according to Haigh?

    b How did she come to be regarded, therefore, as a 'great' Queen?

    c Why do the disagreements about Elizabeth's qualities persist?

5 Read Source 8.

    a In what way does Basnett open up a whole new approach to the interpretation of Elizabeth's reign?

    b In what ways did Elizabeth use the fact that she was a woman to her advantage?

Assessing Elizabeth's achievements

1 Make your own list of Elizabeth's objectives as a monarch.

2 What were Elizabeth's personal qualities?

3 What would you consider to be her failings?

4 What events do you consider were handled successfully by Elizabeth?

5 Which failures of her policy would you think were important?

6 What might have been the judgement of historians if Elizabeth had died in:

   a 1562?

   b 1569?

   c 1588?

A final verdict

But Elizabeth had secured her own future, and bequeathed to James problems which could not be solved: as his failure became clear, her reputation recovered. (Christopher Haigh (ed.), The Reign of Elizabeth I, *Macmillan, 1984)*

Do you agree with this judgement?

FURTHER READING

J. B. Black *The Reign of Elizabeth* (OUP, 1936)

P. Collinson *The Elizabethan Puritan Movement* (1967; Clarendon Press, 1990)

G. R. Elton *The Parliament of England 1559–1581* (CUP, 1986)

M. A. R. Graves *Elizabethan Parliaments* (CUP, 1987)

J. Guy *Tudor Parliaments* (OUP, 1990)

C. Haigh *Elizabeth I* (Macmillan, 1988)

C. Haigh (ed.) *The Reign of Elizabeth I* (Macmillan, 1984)

J. E. Neale *Queen Elizabeth I* (Jonathan Cape, 1935)

J. E. Neale *Elizabeth I and her Parliaments* (OUP, 1953)

A. Somerset *Elizabeth I* (Weidenfeld and Nicolson, 1991)

INDEX

KEY TERMS

Calvinism   26
excommunication   28
historiography   14
monopoly   31
prorogation   22
Protestantism   10
Puritan   30
recusant   43
Reformation   22
transubstantiation   43

PROFILES

Cecil, Robert, Earl of Salisbury   71
Cecil, Sir William, Lord Burghley   36
Devereux, Robert, Earl of Essex   70
Dudley, Lord Robert, Earl of Leicester
   37
Mary Queen of Scots   35
Philip II of Spain   34
Walsingham, Sir Francis   51

MAIN INDEX

Admonition to Parliament   55
Advertisements   54
Alba, Duke of   93
Allen, William   48, 56
Apprentices, Statute of   106
Armada, Spanish   29, 50, 97
'Auld Alliance'   89

Babington Plot   29, 50
Basnet, S   120
Black, J. B.   118
Blois, Treaty of   28, 91
Bond of Association   75
Book of Common Prayer   54–6, 75
Boroughs   22
Bristol, Treaty of   28

Calais   89
Calvin, John   10, 22, 25–7, 52, 75
Camden, William   14–16, 47
Cateau-Cambrésis, Treaty of   22, 34,
   87, 90
Catherine de Medici   91
Catherine of Aragon   8
Catholic League   30, 50, 94

Catholicism, Roman   8–9
Cartwright, Thomas   54, 111
Cecil, Robert   69, 71, 78
Cecil, William   21, 23, 25, 36–8, 43,
   46, 51, 69, 74–8, (Lord Burghley) 87,
   89, 93, 110
Charles I of England   15–16
Civil War, origins of   16–17, 118–9
Clapham, John   3
Cope, Anthony   65, 73
Correction, houses of   105, 109
Currency Reform   25

Dakker, Thomas   11
Darnley, Lord   25–6, 29, 35
De Spes   93
Davies, John   4
D'Ewes, Simonds   101
Devereux, Robert Earl of Essex   32,
   69–70, 118
Device for the alteration of Religion
   38–9, 52
Drake, Sir Francis   92
Dudley, Robert Earl of Leicester   10,
   24, 36–8, 48, 54, 56, 69, 77, 94, 96

Earl of Essex see Robert Devereux
Edinburgh, Treaty of   23
Edward VI   8, 23
Elizabeth I: (her death) 3; (golden age)
   4, 18, Ch 5; (historian's verdicts) 3,
   4, 14–18, Ch 5; (childhood) 8;
   (infatuation with Thomas Seymour)
   9; (image making) 10–13; (protestant
   champion) 10; (virgin queen) 11;
   (parliament) 16, 21, Ch 2; (death)
   32; (marriage) 24–5, 76, 88, 91, 94;
   (excommunication) 27–8, 47, 93;
   (religion) 38–9, Ch 1; (succession)
   76–7
Elton, G. L. R.   16–17, 119
Episcopacy   30, 53, 55, 75
Exchequer   21
Extraordinary Expenditure 67–8

Famine   106, 113–4
France   6–7, 23, 25–6, 28, 34–5, 45,
   49–50, 63, 85, 87, 89–92, 94–7
Francis II   88–9, 91

Graves, M.A.R.   76–7, 80

Green, J.   16
Gresham, Sir Thomas   87
Grindal, Archbishop   30, 45, 55
Guy, J.   119–20

Haigh, C   4, 17–18, 80, 114, 118, 120–1
Harman, Thomas   101
Harrison, William   100–101
Hawkins, Sir John   92–3
Henry VIII   8, 22–3, 119
Henry (IV) of Navarre   30, 34, 50, 71,
   92, 94, 96
High Commission   21
Hill, C   102
Huguenots   26, 28, 49, 63, 90–1

Inflation   105
Ireland   4, 31–2, 70, 90, 93, 118, 120

James I and VI   14–15, 71
Jesuits   49
Jones, N.L.   41
Justices of the Peace   23, 39, 107, 111

Levant Company   95
Lord Lieutenants   22
Lords of the Congregation 89
Luther, Martin   10, 22

Mary Tudor   9, 34, 41, 43, 52
Mary of Guise   23, 35, 88
Mary Queen of Scots   14, 23, 25–9,
   34–5, 64–5, 69, 75, 88, 91
Merchant Adventurers   95
Monopolies   31, 65, 78–9, 97
Mortality rates   114

Naunton, Robert   15–16, 69
Neale, J. E.   16–17, 41, 72–6, 117
Nonsuch, Treaty of   29, 94, 96
North-west passage   92

Ordinary expenditure   67

Parker, Mathew   43, 54–5
Parliament   16–17, 21–2, 24–5, 28, 66,
   Ch 2, 100
Parr Katherine   8
Philip II of Spain   9, 27, 29–30, 34, 46,
   50, 64, 71, 88–90, 92–4
Plague   107, 113–4
Poor Laws   31, Ch 4
Population   102, 108, 113
Poverty   65–6, 102–3, 109
Predestination   26

Prerogative, Court of   21
Presbyterians   30, 54–5
Privy Council   18–19, 22, 49, 66,
   68–71, 75–6, 78–9, 85, 113
Prophesyings   30, 55
Prorogation   22, 65, 68, 75
Protestantism   10, 23–5, 34, 38, 43, 64
Puritans   17, 29–30, 41, 45, 51–6, 74,
   76–7, 111–2
Purveyance   64–5

Raleigh, Sir Walter   78
Recusancy   42–3, 48–50
Reformation   21–2, 40, 91
Ridolfi plot   28
Roman Catholicism   8–10, 15, 18,
   21–5, 29–30, 40, 42–3, 45, 47–9,
   56–7, 64, 72, 91, 93
Rural Disturbances   104, 113

Scotland   6, 14–15, 23, 25–8, 35, 45–6,
   87, 89–91, 95
Seymour, Thomas   9
Smith, A.G.R.   119
Social order   18, Ch 4
Somerset Anne   4, 120
Speaker   68, 72
Star Chamber   21, 56, 78
St. Bartholomew's Massacre 28, 49, 51,
   91
Strickland, William   54–5
Supremacy Act   24, 29, 39, 45, 53, 63

Tawney R.H.   111
Taxes   97, 105
Thiry-nine Articles   75
Throckmorton plot   95
Transubstantiation   42–3, 75
Tyrone, Earl of   31–2

Ulster   31
Uniformity, Act of   24, 39, 41, 63

Vestments   42–3, 64, 75

Wage rates   104, 108
Walsingham, Francis   50–1, 54, 68,
   70, 87, 91
Wentworth, Peter   64–6, 73
Whitgift, John   30, 55
William of Orange   29, 49, 64, 95
Willoughby, John   92
Wool trade   85, 97, 102
Wyatt, Thomas   9